MW00614071

One Million Acres
& No Zoning

Lars Lerup

One Million Acres
& No Zoning

Architectural Association London

I confess that I have not cleared a path through all seven hundred pages, I confess to having examined only bits and pieces, and yet I know what it is, with that bold and legitimate certainty with which we assert our knowledge of a city, without ever having been rewarded with the intimacy of all the many streets it includes.

Jorge Luis Borges

AA Managing Editor: Thomas Weaver
AA Publications Editor: Pamela Johnston
AA Art Director: Zak Kyes
Design: Wayne Daly
Editorial Assistant: Kari Rittenbach

Printed in Belgium by Die Keure

ISBN 978-1-907896-04-0

For a catalogue of AA Publications visit
aaschool.ac.uk/publications
or email publications@aaschool.ac.uk

AA Publications
36 Bedford Square, London WC1B 3ES
T + 44 (0)20 7887 4021
F + 44 (0)20 7414 0783

Contents

For my son Darius

Acknowledgements

This book has been five years in the making, and many manuscripts have appeared in many versions under many titles. But it was not until Edward Dimendberg suggested that I write about my Houston that it was possible to come to any closure. In my earlier versions (all fundamental steps in the process) I want to thank Robert Fishman and Stephen Fox for invaluable editorial advice. My comrades at the Rice School of Architecture John Casbarian, Albert Pope, Carlos Jimenez, Christopher Hight, Sanford Kwinter and Fares el-Dahdah have patiently listened and thoughtfully advised. Aside from the great support provided by Rice University, many other institutions have invited me to lecture, which has allowed me the opportunity to develop and discuss my reading of Houston. Thanks to Roemer van Toorn, Solomon Frausto, Joachim Declerck and Vedran Mimica at the Berlage Institute in Rotterdam; Marc Visser at Megacities in Amsterdam; Richard Foqué and Laura Lee at the ADSL in Antwerp; Douglas Kelbaugh at the University of Michigan who allowed my old friend Peter Calthorpe and I to have a constructive debate on suburban cities; Ralph Lerner at Hong Kong University; Francisco Rodriguez at the University of Puerto Rico; Yung Ho Chang at MIT and the Shenzhen Biennale, China; Alain Bourdin and Didier Rebois at Institut Pour La Ville en Mouvement in Paris; Alfred Jacopy at Anhalt University in Dessau; Karl-Heinz Schmitz at Bauhaus University Weimar; Abelardo Gonzalez at Lund University; Mariluz Barreiros at the Barreiros Foundation in Madrid; Jan Åman at Fargfabriken in Stockholm; Niklas Svensson at Stockholms Stad; Mario Gandelsonas and Stan Allen at Princeton University; Jean La Marche at the University of Buffalo School of Architecture and Planning; Brett Steele at the Architectural Association, London.

11

During the 16 years of my entire Houston Project a cohort of supporters including Aaron Betsky, Sir Peter Cook, Bart Lootsma, Sputnik, Bas Princen, Luis Galliano, Lars Reuterswärd, Maarten Struijs, Joe Powell, Stephen Kleinberg, John Bowles, Paul Winkler, Alfred Jacoby and the late Miles Glaser have encouraged me in various ways in my commitment to explore the suburban city.

I also want to thank Jessica Young and Luke Bulman of Thumb for their earlier work on the graphics and Polly Koch for her editing of an earlier manuscript. I want to thank Stephen Fox – literally my fellow traveller – for his exceptional generosity, profound insight, tireless advice and expertise. Our common trips through Houston followed by lunches in 'dives and palaces' through various sections of the city have been invaluable to this book.

Most importantly, I owe my friend Edward Dimendberg the deepest thanks. Without his unsentimental editing scalpel and insightful guidance, this book would not be a reality.

In the end, writing books is a lonely enterprise, particularly if the task is semi-autobiographical. Supporting institutions provide the security, and often a blind faith in what you are up to. Rice University and its staff – Doris Anderson, Mildred Crocker, Izabel Gass and Hans Krause, Presidents Malcolm Gillis and David Leebron, Provost Gene Levy; and The American Academy in Rome and its staff – director Carmela Franklin, and my friends Peter Campion, Kiel Moe, Jason Moralee, Scott Craver, Terry Adkins and Marty Brody. The Eternal City, with its burden of history and where place still exists, is where the drawings were completed; very distant from Houston Field, its speedways and fleeting loci.

The bets handled by my bookmakers at the Architectural Association – Brett Steele, Thomas Weaver, Kari Rittenbach, Pamela Johnston, Zak Kyes and Wayne Daly – have been more rewarding than any gambler could hope for.

Most of the thumbnail photographs in the Abecedarium are taken by me but there are occasional diagrams done and photographs taken by friends: Jessica Young of Thumb, Aaron Bush, Roemer van Toorn, Bas Princen and George O Jackson. There is also one drawing from the 1940s done by the planner Ralph Ellifrit and one photograph downloaded from the Johnson Space Center website.

Finally, I want to express my deepest affection for my wife, Eva Sarraga de Lerup, whose care and patience carried me through thick and thin.

Lars Lerup
Rome, 12 April 2010

That Thing We Formerly Called the City, or its Theory: Lars Lerup's Houston

Brett Steele

'But it was a neat theory, and he was in love with
it. The only consolation he drew from the present
chaos was that his theory managed to explain it.'
Thomas Pynchon, *V*

If there's any literary justice left in a world where things
formerly called books are still being written, bought and
read in things formerly called the city, then you are thumbing
through this volume's quick-witted sketches and beautiful
layout after having picked it up impulsively from a neatly
arranged, fluorescent-lit rectilinear pile of shrink-wrapped
copies stacked high atop a wooden palette that, along
with hundreds of other offerings left and right, marks out a
shopping aisle running as far as you can see across a concrete
floor of some big-box, no-name discount retailer. Having come
this far, let me do what I can to help you further along with
your accidental discovery – of a big, bright and serious book
written and produced with loving attention to detail, intellect
and insight. It's the product of a real pro. A poet, a
provocateur of the very setting you find yourself otherwise
unable to comprehend. Don't let this book's oblique title, or its
air-conditioned point of sale, tell you otherwise. In the kind of
place where people drive 100 miles for a good fish taco dinner,
or any other remnant of that thing called the city, please judge
this particular book by another measure entirely: its cover –
the one wrapping around its tightly wound argument. These
days covers seem as good a measure as any for judging books,
not to mention cities. Everything inside, I'm happy to confirm,

15

lives up to the package. It's the real deal.

As the cultural capital of an even more interesting (and even less cultured) regional nexus known as Texas, the Houston that serves as our subject here is brought to bright, Homeric, 18-wheeled life in *One Million Acres & No Zoning*. Its author and apologist is one Lars Lerup, who has given us a kind of war memoir set in a place where the non-spaces of late capitalism's battles make the maps hard to read, easy to ignore, and impossible to believe. Lerup pulls no punches, to be sure. But then again, neither does his protagonist – an amorphous, hurricane-arranged settlement of the past century which behaves less like a metropolis than it does a weather pattern: unpredictable, and inhospitable even to its most affectionate forecasters. A locus, one might say, whose genius defeats all but the most abnormal, itinerant forms of analysis.

Think of this book as the insider-ish, partially paranoid monograph that this particular city/non-city has long needed, always feared, and never before been able to imagine. As a collection, the essays achieve the near-impossible: they make Houston relevant to readers far beyond the pipelines and freeways by which it usually defines its own self-importance. A locale filled with a population of bizarre, mechanised migratory patterns and alien forms of cultural exchange; a piece of dusty ground staked out upon fuzzy, overlapping legal claims, set atop teetering, Darwinian development models – all this Lerup bundles together and simply declares it 'Planet Houston'. In so doing, he gets it about right, regarding the evidence Houston offers of extraterrestrial life. Like all good (that is, productive and billable) forms of paranoid schizophrenia, and consistent with the narrative structure of our era's most dominant form of theory (namely, conspiracy theory – of which Houston's larger Texan tabula is most definitely Ground Zero, rather than a prairie home), the

16

following book is as beautiful and picturesque as a ranch spread or a golf course. This is the place JG Ballard always wanted us to get to: a city as pretty as a freeway interchange or electrical substation. (If nothing else, Houston confirms Ballard's well-known aphorism that civilised life is based on a huge number of illusions in which we all collaborate willingly.)

OMA&NZ is a cocktail mix of unexpected observations and flammable diagrams: old-school autobiographical monologue (Philip Marlowe moves to the suburbs) and post-postmodern urban geography (Gilles Deleuze hides out in the frozen food section of a Costco). This is a book with lots of schooling but an unpredictable master – one able to engender the kind of car-wreck fascination that only jaded commuters or nervous critical theorists could ever fully appreciate. Call it the last nail in the coffin of that discipline formerly known as urbanism and you're pretty much there, to the degree that (to adapt a quip about another such place) there really is a there there. The road trip that follows is part of a longer journey that began long before Gertrude Stein set the template with places like Oakland. Ignited a century ago in Baudelaire's deliberately gutter-level view of Paris, embodied soon after in Flaubert's contemporaneous, satirical *Bouvard and Pécuchet*, the analysis of cities through unnatural attention to their most superficial surfaces of the kind embraced by Lerup took an early-modern detour that led us through Kracauer's Berlin and Benjamin's Arcades, to eventually wind up in the New World critical sensibilities of Pynchon's *Crying of Lot 49*, Joan Didion's *Play it as it Lays*, and the business plans of Google Maps. The Houston depicted in Lerup's tale confirms that we've forever left behind not just the golden era of the *flâneur* but also the kind of rear-view mirror mentality recorded by Kerouac, Baudrillard, Ruscha, Scott Brown, Venturi, Koolhaas, et al. As beautifully bound as this latest instalment of this kind of city-as-delirium is, it's one hacked together by knowing its own genealogy so well it becomes little more than a driver's manual – a set of rules for navigating a city best seen from behind the wheel of a large automobile. That such a road tour has come back to its spiritual and petrochemical home, the Oil Capital of the Western World, seems an act as inspired as are its synthetic sunsets.

Urbanism is of course one of those deadly -ism words architects still invoke with the kind of regularity that can only ever be read as a certain kind of discursive insecurity – a nostalgia expressed in a repetition of certain words rather than forms. Underlying a recent and pronounced proliferation of this three-syllable label-as-suffix (note the recent discursive, recursive excess of 'landscape' urbanism, 'ecological' urban-ism, 'typological' urbanism, etc – you get the point), what we find asserted over and over in this invocation of modernisation is the very belief, near religious in its zeal, that architecture remains a world of rational development; in other words, of modern progress and improvement. Boy does that argu-ment come up against a tough opponent in the book you are about to fall into here. If one ever needed a citadel by which to sketch the consequences of capitalism's goofiness much more than its internal contradictions, this book confirms the invitation: Welcome to America's fourth-largest city.

Written and illustrated by a Swedish engineer-turned-architect-flipped-educator, this is a text about a place that Lerup has long embraced with the kind of hug ex-spouses save for one another (heartfelt, but wary) – a place where infrastructural discontinuity, disciplinary uncertainty and critical theory have all been elevated to the status of a personality disorder. It's no coincidence that so many of the beautiful sketches included here have been made with an aerial view: they seem to be looking down on their subject

18

in more ways than one. (Though this elevated vantage point is derived more from the mid-rise condo that Lerup calls home than from any ivory tower that his day job might suggest.)

After reading this book three or four times I've begun to realise that the real ingenuity of *One Million Acres* is something very much the opposite of the contradictory place it chronicles. Unlike Houston, this book is weirdly urbane – an erudite, witty and subversive collage that is as comfortable complexifying as it is demystifying the very incoherence that gives Houston its self-proclaimed identity, its arrogant certainty, and so many other of the qualities that would not recommend it as a subject of serious architectural scholarship. My suggestion is this: read the chapters in any order you want. Skim, jump around, go back to front. Read the same part three times, then leap 20 pages ahead. Use Marshall McLuhan's advice and start on page 69. Let this be a text you travel across just as randomly and unexpectedly as you might in the trip from a car rental lot at the airport to a Mies building next to a mini-mart. In other words, read it like Houston, like the small piece of the kind of city/non-city this book is, and not only adores.

My thanks here to everyone who helped make possible this latest instalment of AA Publications' recent and unexpected books about extraordinary cities. And huge thanks to Lars himself, for keeping alive and malleable this rare form of architectural monograph – one dedicated to a singular site of human aggregation in an age when that pattern is on the rise. Thank you, Lars, for chronicling your planet and for bringing it to us so that we might launch it into orbit from a Georgian Square here in Bloomsbury. And for writing the tale in ways that ease our worries regarding that thing we formerly called the city, or its theory – replaced here by knowledge and experience more meaningful, and lasting, than either.

Foreword

Edward Dimendberg

Houston is the most unexamined of big American cities. Like the edges of civilisation on medieval maps of the earth, there the unnameable begins. Urbanists have studied New York, Boston and Chicago in copious detail, and over the past 20 years even Los Angeles, once anathema, has become a legitimate topic of research. Yet Houston remains startlingly invisible, the pariah of American urban studies and a blind spot in the debate about the future of the city in the United States. You can read most of the serious writing about Houston over the course of a long weekend and still have time to watch that stack of DVDs borrowed from Netflix.

It is not difficult to understand why Houston might prove indecipherable to those accustomed to East or West Coast urbanism and trained in the thinking that predominates in architecture schools there. All of the clichés that once prevailed about Los Angeles – it lacks a centre, is tasteless and nouveau riche and dominated by automobiles – find seeming confirmation in Houston. Throw in a topography without coastal borders, a culture of petroleum, an absence of zoning, a large quantity of churches and it's bound to seem strange, even a little bit scary. Bodies, automobiles and distances appear larger than elsewhere, and the problem of what is real and what is not, where culture begins and nature leaves off, makes California simple by comparison.

That this book, the first sustained engagement with the

1. Georg Simmel, 'The Stranger', in On *Individuality and Social Forms*, edited and translated by Donald N Levine (Chicago, IL: University of Chicago Press, 1971), 143–49.

2. Donald Appleyard, Kevin Lynch and John R Myer, *The View from the Road* (Cambridge, MA: MIT Press, 1965); Robert Venturi, Denise Scott Brown and Steven Izenour, *Learning from Las Vegas* (Cambridge, MA: MIT Press, 1972).

experience of moving through Houston and occupying its spaces, is written by someone who arrived in Houston as an adult, does not strike me as a coincidence. Lars Lerup, a friend from whom I have learned very much about cities, fits the paradigm of sociologist Georg Simmel's Stranger.[1] He, too, came, remained and never stopped looking. Beginning with the view from his apartment window, a kind of lighthouse tower ringed by freeways and condominiums, this book is the record of his apprenticeship to the city. It confirms and documents his insistence on looking at Houston not as an educated European might want it to appear, but in all its messy unruliness. Apostasy comes more naturally to him than to anyone I know.

Lerup is also a disciplinary stranger. There is no single field within which this book comfortably fits. Some architects and urbanists will claim that it lacks a positive programme or design strategy, for which reason they will ignore it. Historians could fault the book for not presenting the city's history through the interpretation of archival materials, social scientists might decry the absence of quantitative data. Furthermore, Lerup refuses to offer his version of what Houston should look like. But to me, these are in fact unique strengths, certifying it to be the product of reflection and observation. Don't even think about importing your own categories and judging Lerup's analyses according to them. Give him the benefit of the doubt, learn his vocabulary and you will likely never view Houston – or any other city – in the same way again. Once all of us learn to see Houston in all of its intricacy, only then can we approach redesigning it.

Lerup is one of the few genuine heirs of the tradition of empirical architectural research into the culture of the

3. Gaston Bachelard, *The Poetics of Space*, trans Maria Jolas (Boston, MA: Beacon Press, 1969), XV.

22

automobile-dominated built environment that commenced with books such as *The View from the Road* and *Learning from Las Vegas*.[2] He deals with Houston in motion – from the interior of a moving automobile, where, like their Los Angeles brethren, Houstonians often find themselves. His notions such as the megashape, holey plane, zoohemic canopy, activity surface and fieldroom sometimes aspire to the status of a generative grammar, a set of rules according to which business districts, suburban enclaves or strip malls might be constructed. More frequently, Lerup's shapes are simply (but hardly simple) records of what he has seen, descriptions and concepts rolled into one.

He is what one might call a no-fuss phenomenologist, seeking what Gaston Bachelard called the 'onset of the image'.[3] Yet he is unwilling to sacrifice rigour. Describing an experience is everything for Lerup; systematising it is less imperative. After years of associating with colleagues in the tradition of environment and behaviour, Lerup denies that normative rules for architectural and urban design exist. We can reconstruct how people make sense of the built environment, but even our best understandings and most plausible theories come up short, and will never automatically deliver better buildings and cities. Inspiration, talent, and careful scrutiny of the environment improve the odds, but for Lerup there are never any guarantees. In his perspective, and in this book in particular, the cheerful optimism of a newcomer to America hangs in precarious balance with a European tragic view of life, with its awareness of human imperfection.

As a city that dispenses with the most significant urban planning instrument – zoning – Houston provides a rich stock of evidence about how people appropriate space in ways never imagined or intended by anyone. Lerup's book, if not his career as a whole, can be understood as a sustained attack on environmental determinism, a reluctance to squeeze laws and testable hypotheses out of Houston. His social science comes without the science but with instead a double helping of the social, which always emphasises the agency of those who occupy and continually remake the city. It reveals neither an unlimited confidence in the wisdom of ordinary Houstonians, nor a belief that politicians, developers or the free market will ultimately arrive at ideal solutions. His willingness to concede that the city might well fail strikes me as a refreshing antidote to the painting-by-numbers approaches to saving the world that proliferate today.

Lerup cannot be bothered with whether the features of Houston he identifies are essential, his methods verifiable, or his insights revelatory of suspiciously mystical *genius loci*. A process of looking infuses his approach, and Lerup is too much the artist for many of his impatient architectural colleagues concerned with building. His drawings fuse Aldo Rossi and Keith Haring with the radiance of *The Wizard of Oz*. Deep in his European heart, Lerup hopes America is the Promised Land. He wrestles with Houston, goes to the mat for better management of its environment and public spaces, yet never denigrates the city. But Lerup has seen more than a few *noir* films (one of our many shared passions) and understands how competition and self-destructiveness play a role in the city he calls home.

This book is a record of his complicated relation to Houston, to which he is not wholly reconciled, but never less than fully engaged. *One Million Acres & No Zoning* is likely to affect Houston in the way that Reyner Banham's *Los Angeles: The Architecture of Four Ecologies* (1972) stimulated more writing about that city's urbanism. The similarities and differences between the books and their authors are revealing. Both Banham and Lerup grew up in Europe – in Britain and

Sweden, respectively. Both received training as engineers, yet increasingly gravitated toward cultural questions. Banham lived in Los Angeles for brief periods of time, mostly while teaching at the University of Southern California. Lerup has lived in Houston since 1992. Each argues for the exceptional-ism of his adopted city and both find the break up of Georgian estates in nineteenth-century London a striking precedent for sprawling urban expansion. Each apprehends his city by automobile and recognises how this inflects the quality of everyday life.

Yet here the similarities end and profound differences between Banham and Lerup emerge. Banham is an aesthete whose book treats landmark modernist buildings by Frank Lloyd Wright, Richard Neutra, Rudolf Schindler, Charles and Ray Eames and Craig Ellwood. One searches in vain for a comparable list in Lerup's book, which makes no mention of the work of modernist architects such as Philip Johnson, John Burgee, Renzo Piano, Mies van der Rohe, Cesar Pelli and Gunnar Birkerts, who have all built in Houston, let alone newcomers like Carlos Jimenez. You will read this book in vain if you seek to learn about Lerup's taste or the city's architectural landmarks. But if you crave a description of a leaf-blower as funny as anything Kafka ever wrote, you've come to the right place.

Banham sought to understand the style of Los Angeles architecture and design to determine how the city has left its impact on the world. By contrast, Lerup neither passes judgement on Houston, nor elevates its commercial vernacular to an authentic populism, as Venturi, Scott Brown and Izenour did in their study of Las Vegas. He is not interested in architectural aesthetics at the level of buildings and does not concern himself with the catalogue of styles one finds in guidebooks. His crosshairs are trained on the urban region

25

of Houston in all of its mind-bending complexity.

Lerup never explicitly develops a normative account of the city, except at its most environmentally dysfunctional. This can sometimes make the experience of reading rather frustrating, until one grasps that energy usage, ecological sustainability and the availability of public space and services are the criteria by which Lerup judges Houston – and often finds it wanting. To paraphrase Richard Rorty, one might claim Lerup believes that once the larger systemic challenges are addressed and resolved, the truth and beauty of Houston will take care of itself. Few Europeans would so willingly dispense with an underlying metaphysics, and in this way Lerup reveals the pragmatic American grain of his approach to the city.

So, too, Banham and Lerup differ on their understandings of ecology, which for Banham has more to do with aesthetics, mood and style than the concerns of environmentalism. Of all the ways in which *Los Angeles: The Architecture of Four Ecologies* has aged, its refusal to address the politics of energy in suburban car culture is perhaps most conspicuous. As forest fires, floods and mudslides become ever more common in Los Angeles, the ecologies in Banham's book appear increasingly rigid and ill equipped to address the problems of density and infill that chiefly concern Lerup. Writing at a moment when global warming, climate change and hurricanes impact Houston, Lerup is sensitive to overbuilding, the replacement of vegetation by concrete and the destruction of the local bayous.

Dialogue amongst members of architecture schools and real-estate developers is today no longer as rare as it once was. Lerup's reports of conversations with Bob Schultz, Frank Liu and Richard Everett provide revealing insights into Houston's ongoing expansion and go a long way toward expunging the ludicrously simplistic view that they are the bad guys on whose doorsteps all blame for its urban problems can be laid. If Lerup's commitment to a public realm distinguishes him from most libertarians, his lack of faith in state-implemented solutions just as clearly suggests that improvements in Houston will not come about as the consequence of new government programmes, but rather as a consequence of hard-won collaborations among citizens, architects, politicians and real-estate interests.

After the financial crisis of 2009–10 which left the Californian model of prosperity in tatters, there is good reason to view Houston and the general strength of the Texas economy as a possible model for the future. Any prospect for the city that is more hopeful than ecological catastrophe, as well as politically feasible, must assume that capitalism will not disappear soon and that it in fact *must* be an agent of creative transformation. Here again, Lerup demonstrates his willingness to think outside of familiar categories. How the continuing experiment of Houston will unfold is uncertain, yet without a doubt, no book that will teach me more about the city than this one is likely to appear within my lifetime.

Introduction

In 1966 I made my first trek to the United States, travelling from Stockholm to New York. On the subsequent drive cross-country, my interest in American urbanism begins. Here long vistas – the big sky I previously associated with the North Sea – appear over the land. Cities and towns are dispersed in surrounding vastness. Houses seem to have escaped their foundations and to be themselves on the move.[1]

Once I arrive in California to augment my Swedish engineering degree with an architectural education at the College of Environmental Design at UC Berkeley, my interest in suburbia develops further, at first obscurely, through forays into San Francisco Bay Area suburbs at the behest of two sociology teachers. Early in the summer of 66, in the midst of Berkeley's brewing student revolution, I work as a draftsman for Claude Oakland on the now famous Eichler homes. Oakland is his last architect. Perhaps inspired by the times, I become enamoured with Eichler's progressivism. Much later I return to teach at Berkeley, and only after 15 years of introducing American urbanisation to thousands of undergraduates in a course on 'People & Environment' does suburbia etch itself onto my mind for good. Yet it is not until my encounter with Houston in 1993 that the spectacular drama of suburbanisation becomes lived experience. It dawns on me that, until then, I had never really been in America.

In the discontinuous suburban conurbations of Houston, the most startling encounters between nature and culture transpire. Trees and houses face each other in simultaneous

1. Decades later, after reading JB Jackson's 'Westward-moving House', I realise I was not entirely wrong. See: 'The Westward-moving House' in Erwin H Zube (ed), *Landscapes: Selected Writings of JB Jackson* (Boston, MA: University of Massachusetts Press, 1970), 10–42.

conflict and amorous alliance – yet the persistent demonising of this form of co-habitation inhibits reflection. Under the rubric of *sprawl,* many contemporary critics approach suburban cities with disdain, sarcasm, dismissal. This treatment inspired my contrarian nature and led me to look closer.

Forty years since I first encountered it, suburbia continues to fascinate me. Flat, regimented and strangely forlorn, it rushes by through the window of Continental Flight 60 from Houston to Stockholm via Newark's Liberty, reminding me of my own itinerancy, of my carbon footprint. I find myself engaged in my own version of Stockholm syndrome, in which hostages eventually side with their captors. Like my ancestors, who for centuries were captive to the ocean (despite a tendency to seasickness), I too have been hijacked. But this time by the vastness of the suburban dream, and despite my occasional queasiness, willingly so.

At first view Houston is a prototypical American city, located roughly in the bottom centre of the huge rectangular landmass that forms the United States. But Houston is a special case: it is motorised, broken up and attenuated from the very start. It does not follow the typical escape scenario of expansion in cities like New York or Chicago. At its inception, Houston already leaves the traditional city behind. Mobility – the embodiment of an eternal restlessness – drives this vast suburb. It provides a blueprint for abandoning the centralised city, rendering an old model superfluous. Aside from its current polycentricity, Houston's seemingly inevitable trajectory was eerily predicted by the city's first postwar planner, Ralph Ellifrit, in his 'Theoretical City' of 1948. There is no suburban city more raw or revealing of what happens when land planners and builders (and later, real-estate developers) operate in cahoots with city officials, abetted by various federal and local regulations, no zoning, rudimentary

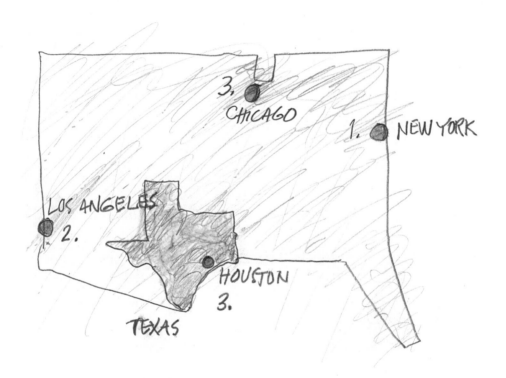

Houston, Texas and the US

planning instruments, market intelligence, technology, labour and plenty of capital.

Although they look alike, Houston is very different from the Los Angeles that I once knew well. Houston began as a motorised city, Los Angeles did not. Californians built it around a rail system that motorisation later defeated, and much of the original organisation of the city can still be discerned. Los Angeles is at least four times denser than Houston, confined by a topographical bowl. Houston is endless. Los Angeles develops next to the ocean, Houston 50 miles from it. Los Angeles has zoning, Houston doesn't. Houston is wet and humid, spreading around a delta of bayous, always ready to flood. Los Angeles is a dry city that buys its water from far away.

Where did Houston come from? Apart from the moist prairie and bayous that I have grown to love, Houston takes all of its urban developmental cues from elsewhere.[2] Although the popularity of suburbia dates back to Georgian London of the seventeenth and eighteenth centuries (where, according to Robert Fishman, London's West End streets and squares marked the 'real origins of the capitalist subdivision process'),[3] little of this 'bourgeois charm' remains in the cookie-cutter turboscape of today's suburb. Surreptitiously, the old 'charm' that evoked a communal city in those original squares – houses encircling a common green space – disappears en route to Houston. It is lost in translation.

Houston's suburbia shifts directly to the house in the garden, leaving all other accoutrements behind. An escape from confinements more abstract than those of the traditional city – cultural history, family, inherited destinies – may have

2. Houstonians with a long memory are less enamoured with the bayous, remembering that they were once delivery channels for yellow fever, 'snakes and vermin'.

3. Robert Fishman, *Bourgeois Utopias: The Rise and Fall of Suburbia* (New York: Basic Books, 1987), 18–38.

encouraged the process. Houston is never a destination but always a point of departure, the exhilarating beginning for a steady flow of newcomers. It seems perfectly reasonable to find the space programme located here – a launch pad for the last frontier.

All of us have a unique view of the city we inhabit. But some cities are more conducive to undisturbed personal perception than others. Houston is such a city – the absence of shared space sees to this. Predominantly motorised and individualised, Houston limits pedestrian and public experience to interior spaces – be it mall, arena, church or parking garage – where the city is always beyond the horizon. Exterior space is dominated by the movement through it; whether parking tarmac, freeway, cloverleaf, frontage road, cul-de-sac. Houston is mine (and everybody else's), rarely to be shared, merely an extension of my driveway.[4] You are the lone ranger.

In my travels across Houston I often find myself wishing for a different city, not out of disaffection, but out of affection for what the city *promises* – an Open City, less gated, more public and more like the moist prairie it occupies. This book is a record of the journeys, fantasies, nightmares, speculations and hopes provoked by the city that I call home. Many of the phenomena it describes can be found in other contemporary American cities; thus the book doubles as an account of a more pervasive condition, a transition from the traditional city to a more unruly mode of contemporary space whose subjects and dynamics I treat as entries in a lexicon.

Texas is well established as the energy capital of the United

4. There is another side to this solipsistic view of the city. It is the 'city of neighbourhoods' where civic organisation, often around contentious issues, comes into being only to disappear when the disturbance has passed. A city that is not directly visible (although its consequences may be), it can only be experienced. Or as in my case, overheard. This is part of what I will refer to later as self-organisation.

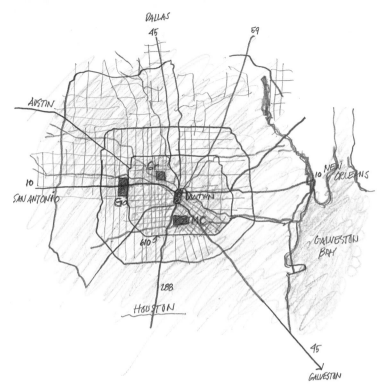

Greater Houston

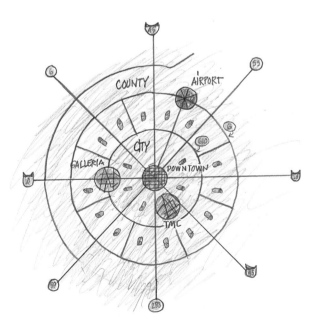

Houston: Inner Loop

States. Its political clout is equally well known; many native daughters and sons have served in Washington. And then there is size. Driving across the state, one crosses a third of the country. In the midst of the current recession, its economic significance has grown, particularly in light of California's bankruptcy. Here the so-called Texaplex – a triangle whose points are defined by San Antonio, Dallas and Houston, and whose interior includes Fort Worth and Austin – suggests a new state geometry housing 80 per cent of the population.

The three corner cities are often caricatured in popular imagination. Little factual information manages to float to the surface: San Antonio is margaritas and mariachis on a river walk. Dallas is still mourning JR's departure and Houston is a desert with oil derricks in the backyard. Behind these stereotypes, San Antonio serves as the NAFTA gateway to Mexico and beyond, while Dallas houses a vast financial centre (and a giant airport). That Houston is about to surpass Chicago in size to become the third largest city in the country is dismissed as an anomaly of a vast and flat suburbia. But if one looks closer, Houston may well be the most democratic city in the union. It has a culturally and demographically broad population with a vast pool of housing at reasonable prices. It offers a huge labour market with an economy diversified far beyond energy, but not entirely unrelated to it, and one of the world's great medical centres. As California's extensive government services (propped up by a highly evolved taxation structure) begin to collapse, Houston steps forth as the place and mind to understand (if not aspire to). With its immense and flat playing field, the city is a creature of the market – the same market that was invented to create an even playing field to remedy the vagaries of both social and economic justice. And it is a city in perpetual transit; the exemplary expression of Marc Augé's supermodernity – a mélange of places and non-places where history is light and speed as dominant as time.[5] Perhaps more mundanely, Houston has no zoning: a fact that would make any respected urbanologist go apoplectic: 'It's just Sprawl!' In this sense, *One Million Acres & No Zoning* aspires to be a provocative and timely addition to the emerging literature on urbanism, or better still, supermodernism.

My 16-year search for Houston is drawing to a close. The first instalment, *After the City* (1998),[6] derived its title from a certain level of bewildered excitement which made it both inspired and naïve. This inspiration remains and so too the naiveté. Yet today they are of a different magnitude, tempered by awe and the realisation that anyone who studies a city of this size will never fully know it – the conurbation remains as mysterious as the humanity that occupies it. One million acres of human occupation, without zoning, is conceptually so large, so complex and so intriguing that the city emerging from these pages will seem quite different from the post-city of my first volume. Contemporary Houston is neither city nor metropolis, but an urban condition of a third kind.

5. Marc Augé, *Non-Places: An Introduction to Supermodernity* (New York: Verso, 2008).
6. Lars Lerup, *After the City* (Cambridge, MA: MIT Press, 2001).

A New City?

A cluster of towers pokes through the relentless flatness of a suburban field. Will it be a new city, usurping suburbia and folding it into the sloppy embrace of an endless urbanisation? The din of freeway drowns the thought.

Under a green canopy, suburbia dozes in the summer heat. We are in Houston but we could be in any number of American cities. We came here to commune with nature. We thought that gardening amongst winding streets and cul-de-sacs would bind us to our new home. But we came here with our city ways, our technologies and a tendency to view all material as discrete building blocks: brick, tree, grass (trucked in on flatbeds). The result may be even more artificial than the city we left behind. Ours is a bogus nature that can only be maintained with leaf-blowers and fertilisers, not to speak of the automobiles that shuttle us back and forth to central nodes. Does the new city emerge here?

Radical changes taking place before our eyes in human settlements suggest that we must reassess modern urbanisation. For the first time in history there are no clear categories or simple binary oppositions, but a complex bio-technical diversity that is spreading and affecting everything: cities, regions, nations, the world. As an architect I find myself drifting further and further away from my profession in search of a new, accommodating practice, sampling concepts and vistas from philosophy and geography. Just as Robert Irwin claimed that from the day his painter's brush slipped outside the canvas he could never return to its flat confines, neither can I return to the pretty facade or clever house plan.[1]

There are two streams to the freeway: one towards the outer suburbs, the other back to the city. These directions are easily confused with the back and forth of the daily commute.

1. Recounted by Robert Irwin in a lecture at Rice University, March 1994.

Those moving outwards may be in the search of that 'other city', even beyond the rural, and those moving inwards bound for 'the city on the hill'. Yet both trajectories still depend on petroleum, the elixir of modernisation. But since the petroleum era has a distinct finality, if only projected, both streams nourish utopian speculations: the latter amongst the cluster of towers – the *Dense City* – and the former in the interstices between (now outmoded categories of) nature and culture – the *Green City*.

What is Suburbia?

Hiding behind the old nomenclature in the chiaroscuro of future possibilities, Houston is still a sprawling suburban city. But its constant transformation implicitly questions this outworn label, although in most eyes it still sprawls. Most probably it will continue to do so, especially for those who do not care to look closely. But beyond the rhetoric of sprawl is a much more challenging question: What is suburbia? It cannot just be a freeway and a set of sprawling subdivisions. Is it a long commute by car? A one-storey attenuated conurbation of discrete objects set upon an essentially flat surface? Such shorthand descriptions are too glib and too close to the urban intellectual's to have any purchase on the real suburbia. The mixture of graphic simplicity and cultural ambiguity suggests the need for a very different reading of the typical subdivision. We usually only see suburbia from above, at a deceptive distance that allows us to reject it as sprawl. To tell its story we must not only roam the freeway but also follow those automobiles leaving the cloverleafs beyond the commercial strip, and disappearing into the stillness of the subdivision, its innermost lair. This is where we will find the 'new bourgeoisie' living in utter abundance, at least for the moment. We will also discover a vast assembly of *topoi* – places – switching on and off as if controlled by a large circuit board. Stim and dross. Suburbia is a state of orchestrated flux, as if the combustion powering cars on the motorway reverberated far beyond initial firing. Most importantly, we will find that the suburban city, more than any other urban condition, is already the graphic representation of our most urgent dilemma: a provocative confrontation with nature.

Middles

Then is the suburban city a mere conflation of opposites? Or is it even more ambiguous, as suggested by the identification of several other formations such as *metropolis*, and lately *megalopolis* and *megacity*? None seems to describe Houston. Somewhat frustratingly, I have here attempted to find suitable monikers: 'vast, attenuated conurbation', or 'discontinuous city', or 'turboscape'. None are particularly appealing. When the unit of occupation is the form of the pavilion – a singular object surrounded by open space – we can no longer fully separate building from landscape. A single-family house without a lawn is not a home. In turn, this suggests that in the spectrum from densely packed city to the semi-wilderness of a vast prairie, Houston (as its sister cities) forms *a middle landscape*, suspended between the two. This in-between condition was beautifully captured by John Updike, when he told Jane Howard of *Life Magazine* in 1966:

> I like middles, it is in the middles that extremes clash, where ambiguity restlessly rules.

43

Green City

The extreme ambiguity and restlessness to which Updike refers are not only reflected in lives lived in the middle, but in the very organisation of space. The extremes of habitation and nature clash, resulting in profound ambiguity: Are sprawling houses for or against nature? Is nature mere backdrop to the good life? Does nature have a say and, if so, is it easily held in place by lawnmowers and leaf-blowers? Are suburbanites really living in and with nature, or are they just 'up against' it? Such questions are not easily answered. And the physical obscurity resulting from the relentlessly disrupted, jagged and apparently unorganised – the holey plane – produces a further ambiguity of place and location. Sign and road, rather than space, show the way. A bastard urbanism, growing hysterically in what Alain Badiou calls 'the rump century' – the 30 years between 1970 and 2000.

Nomadic Urges

Where do all the highways go?
Now that we are free.

When Canadian songwriter and poet Leonard Cohen sings these lines, the middle landscape floods my thoughts. Where does the vast 'suburb' lead? Is it blinded by desire to escape the traditional city, without giving a thought to where all its highways would stretch? And Cohen's second line, 'Now that we are free' – free from what? The old city and its insistent community, its crowding, its ethnicities, its purported decadence, its diseases, its lack of green space, light and air? For those who never fled but have only known suburbia, now the new city, where do their highways end? In a cul-de-sac, too? Now that the era of escape is long-gone, what drives the

45

pursuit of total mobility? Of freedom? Cohen's provocation may be more relevant than ever today.

Since the Second World War, nations accustomed to migrations have witnessed an unexpected addition to the ancient trek from hinterland to city. It marks a change in both direction and speed. This additional movement is not *to* but *from* the city, made not by the poor or other fortune-seekers but by an emerging middle class who pack their cars, or fill train and tram compartments, in a rush to the new suburbs. If we continue to consider the emerging middle class shift to suburbia as an escape from the city – a movement away from something reprehensible – nomadism would have little bearing on the matter. But what if the tendency reflects an embedded nomadic itinerancy? The same urge that drove us to recognise the link between the metabolism of the horse and the powers of the combustion engine. Or the conceptual leap that built the automobile? It is an itinerancy that has nothing to do with escape and everything to do with mobility, an urge that has driven Americans perpetually to wander not only in search of something better, but as the expression of a genetic disposition as ancient as fleeing from predators in the aboriginal forest.

The keys to this 'nomadic momentum' are motorisation and electronic communication. These two modes of 'propulsion', made possible by complex advancements in microchip technology, are allowing humans to not only move their bodies but their ideas (and money) at a dizzying speed. Suburbia is being urbanised (Los Angeles) and the city radically suburbanised (Detroit), while metropolitan regions are becoming more important than either. Los Angeles may be the most evolved example of the new city, while Houston is its frontier. Here, the well-known graphics of post-war suburbia clash with the churning pulsations of an increasingly flexible real-estate machine; predatory in some eyes, beleaguered in others. Here, the somnolent subdivision sits in a booming freeway domain. Here, the space programme and monster trucks burn fuel at astronomical rates while the lone bicyclist or jogger minimally contributes to the energy crunch, although inhabiting the same flatness. The old *topoi* appear in increasingly surprising combinations, invisibly manipulated by virtual forces. Local economies are no longer local, regional, statewide or national but now global, too. Community, culture and events are likewise dispersed and disembodied. No longer embedded in the ensemble of rider–horse–steppe, the new nomads are simultaneously distorted and enhanced by a galaxy of technology, their bodily connection to the suburban setting merely incidental.

To investigate a nomadic trajectory in suburbia is to consider all forms of mobility, essential when nothing is ever still, or at least not for very long. Always slippery, the 'new city' cannot be categorically defined, for it is continually in transition. Language is much of the problem since it relies so heavily on difference, while the 'new city' operates according to a logic of 'both/and' that cannot be held in place. It must be caught in flight.

The Wandering Polis

Sigmund Freud led me to it. Reading *The Interpretation of Dreams* while working on a conceptual project 'with a pretty facade and clever house plan' in the 1980s, I realised that the city itself hides behind the facade of a house. (Much later, I understood that nature also hides behind the city, and actually in suburbia.) In this sense the barrier between the architect and the world was forever broken for me. The previously

47

Suburban Houston with Downtown on the Horizon

stable facade of the suburban house – securely held in place by the history of architectural classicism – is today a screen at best. Encountering the same houses, clustered in broken down huddles in the shadow of a refinery along the Houston Ship Channel, the tripartite screen fades. Poverty and pollution levels, cancer rates, employment data attach themselves like speech-bubbles, turning the house into a mere scaffold for statistics. Landing at Hobby Airport after dark, the huddles fade to black, actually and symbolically overshadowed by the refinery's pyrotechnics.

Every time I fly over the United States at night, I am struck by its vastness and haunting seductiveness, while humbled by the challenge to understand it. Clusters of light (city?) everywhere, each punctuated by a unique distance (nature?), in darkness shading both purpose and thought. In Perry Miller's *Errand into the Wilderness*, one appreciates that (after overcoming the oceans and subsequent distances between the Puritans and their others: Baptists, Anabaptists, Native Americans, etc) this peculiarly American Distance is a unique cultural accomplishment. The distance separating all these lights when seen from above signifies the desire of a transient culture, forever running to the next stop. In my native Sweden, moving constituted failure, but here in the deep shadows between the lights, moving is success. Such is the balm of the émigré: escape and 'moving on' are frequently confused.

In America, the traditional city poorly served the middle class, or so it seems from the escape narrative and its complaints of crime, poverty, ethnic diversity, economic disparity and inferior schools. Newly acquired wealth, government subsidies, motorisation and speed all provide impetus to leave, yet since jobs stay behind, the new suburbanites return by daily commuting back and forth between the new territories and the old city. From a nomadic perspective, continuous displacement emerges as a value. Even in the thick of the commute, the lone driver dominates. A road warrior, with news and coffee close to hand. Back and forth, maybe unconsciously dreaming of drifting further west. (Is it surprising that most suburban expansions are to the west?)

Umbilically connected, the traditional city and suburbs share an essential metropolitan identity. In both, artifice dominates nature, even if the building material is crabgrass. Although physically distinct, the dominating urbanity of the city and the dominating landscape of the suburb have been fused by mobility. (A mobility that came late to our civilisation, but which now dominates it.) It is a fusion that turns the building blocks of nature (crabgrass) and culture (houses) into mere stepping stones in the endless back and forth of a roaming population.

The smoothness of Houston's original moist prairie was at first discreetly lined by houses and roads, but once mechanisation took command lines were drawn deeper, more permanent. Add to this the commute itself – and all the side-trips – and the smooth becomes striated. Mobility, as a form of overwriting, submits everything to artifice. Literally tattooed, the smooth body of the land is now overrun by illustrations. Its horizon broken, its shape and subtle turns erased, its microclimates shattered, man's writing criss-crosses the ancient prairie, dominating the smooth. The binary opposition between city and suburb is dead. A new urban genus – simultaneously local and global, tiny and vast, simple and complex, city and suburb – is rising from its ashes.

Only by riding this new organism is it possible to appreciate it. Let us be nomads and take the cul-de-sac for what it is: a vortex that again and again throws one back into the world. As the conclusion of suburban escape, the cul-de-sac is at best misanthropic, dull, comforting,and at worst the tail-end of a

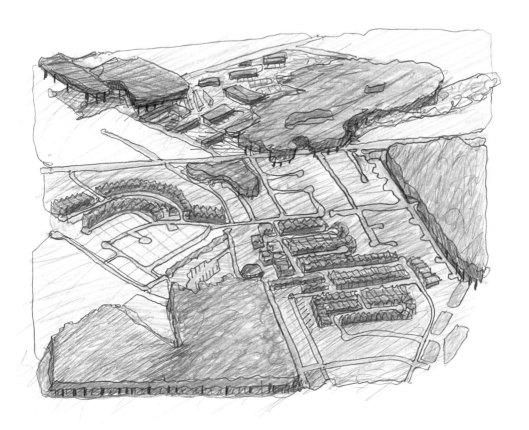

Suburban Fragmentation

bold experiment in habitation. Driving through Houston, and with lesser frequency Los Angeles, Phoenix and Newark, I began to realise that the urbanisation now taking place not only defies old categories but suggests new qualities in the making. Yet these facts are not associated with the architecture or the people who I drove by, but with the roving atmosphere of the entire conurbation – the streaming itself. This streaming that affects everything from real-estate transactions to human interactions comprises a new condition, in which the ancient stability of the city has been exchanged for its opposite.

In the traditional city people move regimentally by way of the extensive grid system, through compartmentalised interiors, corridors, assemblies of confining spaces and arrays of rooms. But when Houstonians ride the city, smoothness dominates. A centrifugal force propels them along the swirling highways, deceptively transgressing underlying obstacles, crossing territory in the blink of an eye. Drivers move as if storm or wave propels them in perpetual displacement. But this is speed confused as smoothness. Because when halted at one of many singularities – traffic light, typical suburban house or shopping centre – the driver is reminded that space is still striated and confinement and closure once again replace speed. The apparent smoothness of the speeding driver's world (idealised by the nomad's trail through a seemingly endless desert) is here diverted, parcelled out of smoothness-as-speed.[2]

The real smoothness slumbering in the bend of an untouched bayou or ancient prairie, skipped over by the real-estate machine, seems forever hidden and blissfully forgotten. The outline of a question is beginning to form:

2. Gilles Deleuze and Felix Guattari, *A Thousand Plateaus*, trans Brian Massumi (London: Continuum, 2004), 380.

Must we return to smoothness? Do we need the smooth turnings of nature to connect our own diminished bodies with our inflated minds? Do speed and defensible space compensate for the abandonment of ancient smoothness? (Is it worth it?)

While a truly nomadic field would be utterly smooth, the actual field is a peculiar contradiction of speed and confinement – a truly schizophrenic proposition emblematic of the 'American Dream', of having 'my own house, close and accessible to the world but also separated and protected from the parts I don't care for'. Such territoriality scars people and space. But the nomadic impulse exacerbates this contradiction through its propensity for incessant movement.

Looking at a typical subdivision, we see the centrifugal pattern of little houses circling a virtual fire.[3] This mathematics of house and site – of patterned behaviour, point and plane – is a peculiarly American phenomenon (although outliers can be seen in the Venix projects occupying the Green Heart of the Dutch Randstad, in suburbs in Germany and China, as well as the Garden Cities of England.) It is a socio-physical mathematics of simultaneously overcoming and making distance, which seems to originate from the Puritans' first forest clearing.

Planet Houston

Beginning with the four dispatches that Amerigo Vespucci wrote about his trips back and forth to the New World, the myth of America as a land enchanted beyond all others has emerged. This sense of uniqueness has lasted more than 500 years – not a bad run for a persistent mythology. Jean

3. Ibid, 362.

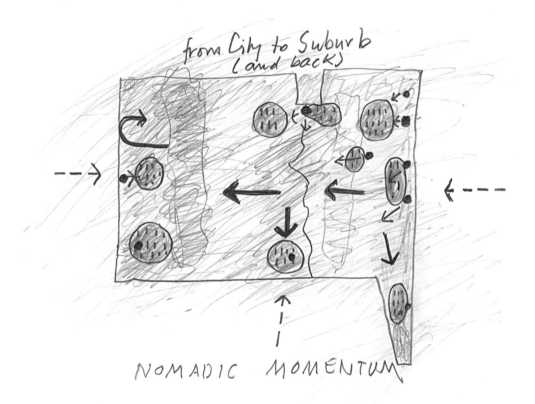

Nomadic Momentum

Baudrillard put it clearly, if somewhat paternalistically, when he suggested that America was Planet Europe's satellite. What is startling about the power of this myth is how many buy into it on both sides of the divide.[4] Because of its peculiar geographical relationship to Europe and its opportune appearance as the final leg on the global trajectory, America became the place for dreams that had previously existed without an actual locus – as mere literary speculation, as utopia. There was a paradise on earth and America was it! And it has retained some of this conceptual allure, especially for Europeans. Yet once they populated the country, Americans rarely wrote about utopia. On the ground, things change. For Europeans, America fulfilled the last essential part of the world map, presaging the creation of the modern object *par excellence* – earth itself – as globalisation became the last expression of Western expansion toward conceptual completeness.[5]

America remains the ultimate expansion of the Western mind: it is still the 'universe of the extreme', a site for regressive fantasies – a type of double exile, from Europe as well as from itself, and at the same time an actual place firmly on the world map.[6] The result is a much more complex America than any of the more or less explicitly utopian projections performed by European (mostly French) visitors to the golden land. After Vespucci, the utopian trajectory was resumed in earnest by Alexis de Tocqueville's short visit to nineteenth-century America. Ostensibly on a fact-finding mission to study

---

4. Gisle Selnes' 'Exilia, Utopia, America: Et bidrag til eksilets utopografi' ('Exile, Utopia, America: A Note on the Utopography of Exile') *Vagant* 1, 2004 (http://www.vagant.no/article/45767) is an inspired clarification of the sources of the utopian atmosphere surrounding America. Still prevailing in various forms, he writes: '*Fra foerste stund tar Amerika plassen som utopiens kontinent gjennom en systematisk resirkulering av topoi som har vaert i bruk i tradisjonelle fremstillinger av absolutt velvaere… Amerika er en ny oppfinnelse: oppfinnelse av det nye.*' ('From the first instant, America took the place of the utopian continent through a systematic recirculation of topoi that were used in traditional descriptions of total bliss… America is a new invention: the invention of the new.')

5. Ibid, 4.

6. Ibid, 5.

the American penitentiary system, he also wrote *Democracy in America*. But he wrote from a very specific perspective, at the same time detached and impassioned, revealing that he was still an aristocrat despite his 'democratic' ambitions – a leaning perhaps best revealed by his choice of American informants, largely an elitist group of 'upper-class lawyers and Federalists'.[7] This bias was reinforced by the political situation at the time, which presented a window of opportunity for the Federalists who, after a long decline, had won the 1796 election. Tocqueville's obsession with the 'tyranny of the majority' may stem from this: he ultimately favoured dispersed state governance. Here the utopian format found a focus in succinct rationalisations – marked in his case by brilliance and erudition – yet, as is always true in model-making, prone to oversimplification and misrepresentation. But others have followed Tocqueville's lead: Reyner Banham, Jean Baudrillard and Bernard Henri-Lévy may be the most prominent.[8] All of them remain controversial and yet beguiling, larded in utopian hopes and disappointment. America remains a vessel that will never live up to its promise, but it also remains the only means to reach that seductive and ultimate idyll of Arcadia. As long as Planet Europa exists, America will be its favourite satellite. No China or India will replace it, despite enormous economic potential. Their history and actual problems are all too real, unlike America's, viewed from afar as bold projections or even utopian experiments. Even in times such as these when America seems to have lost all credibility, and those outside pronounce the utopia finally expired, hope remains for those of us who live on the endless prairie.

It is in the spirit of planetary exploration, at the helm of

7. Colin Kidd, 'A Matter of Cast', *London Review of Books* 22 (March 2007), 29–30.

8. See Reyner Banham, *Los Angeles: The Architecture of Four Ecologies* (New York: Harper and Row, 1971); Bernard Henri-Lévy, *American Vertigo* (New York: Random House, 2006).

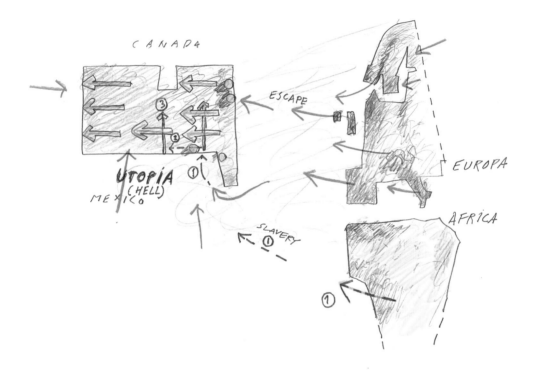

Utopia, Europe & Africa

a nomadic rover, that we will explore Houston, viewing it no longer as a sprawling suburban city but as an emerging 'middle landscape': a new city rich with opportunity, complexity, contradictions and daunting challenges. This newness does not resemble the projections of a truly new city – either dense or green – but rather comes from a constant and relentless transformation that renews the city every day. In Houston, we never step into the same bayou twice. Houston is truly unique, and yet so much like all other suburban metropoles on the North American continent. Yet when seen from this perspective Houston appears to be a city of a third kind. If not exactly extraterrestrial, it clearly leaves the old city behind in the dust, while vigorously negating my early notion of Houston as a metropolis.[9]

And who are the denizens of a third kind? As Alain Badiou has shown, at the centre of the twentieth-century struggle for the real, the communist's new man had to succumb to the collective – where he and she also bit the dust – while the fascist's new men failed miserably as the strutting automatons of the master race.[10] Simultaneously, quietly, almost surreptitiously, a new man spread out on the American prairies, largely obscured from the Eurocentric point of view. He and she (meticulously constructed by capital, industry and government) have matured into suburban man toiling in the seductive euphoria of consumption. His multicultural species are the denizens of the third kind, now facing their own struggle of survival.

9. My conversion has been greatly enhanced in conversations with Albert Pope, who puts it simply: 'a metropolis is a contiguous metropolitan area'. One cannot say this of Houston.

10. Alain Badiou, *The Century* (Cambridge, MA: Polity Press, 2007), 98–110.

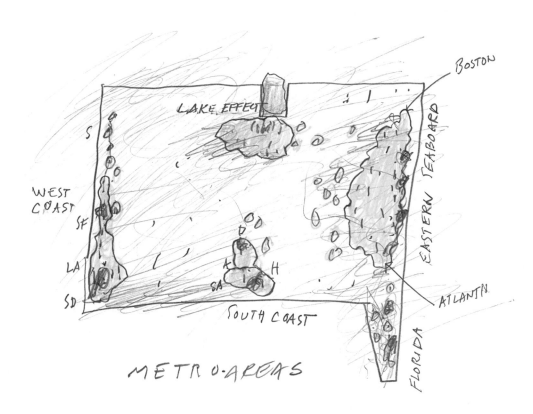

METRO-AREAS

Nomadic Momentum

OBJECTS

EVENTS

POPULATIONS

MEDIUM

...Beyond EVENTS

RJ SUBSTRATE

...beyond OBJECTS

Time
Geography

The restless middle landscape lies before us. It defies anything but crude understanding through two favoured perspectives: the view from the air and the view from the road. Unlike the traditional city's 24-hour activity, pockets of inactivity permeate. When stillness appears, darkness engulfs movement and provides contrast when the switch is flicked back on. Stim and dross are the basis of metropolitan dispersion.[1] From above, the city appears roughly divided in two, shared equally by nature and culture – landscape and built-up area. (In time and closer up we shall see that this binary vision is all too crude.) In the traditional city, landscape is mere affectation. Juxtaposition is what characterises the middle landscape. Here the house is not, as in the city, central to its structure and organisation – its very architecture – but sidelined, put out to pasture in the garden. Despite its symbolic importance, in the suburban city the house is out of focus, making the in-between the conceptual pivot around which life turns. Distance is the fundament of this organisation of space.

The sense of dispersion must have been even greater in early Houston. We can speculate that overcoming distance to seek community and services was more urgent than making distance to ensure privacy. In Texas ample space is a given, and Houston's snake- and insect-infested delta of bayous possibly the only release from endless prairie. It is no surprise that there were more cars in Houston in the early twentieth century than in any other American city. Eastern cities, from where most newcomers came, were still railroad suburbs and largely pedestrian. In Houston distance became a daily preoccupation. Increasing density steadily encroaches on the

1. The same discontinuity that the US Strategic Bombing Survey saw as antidote to fear and destruction in the atomic age. Houston remains the ideal expression of sentiments set forth in the 1945 survey, in which its authors argued for 'protection through space' by means of dispersing all military targets. See: Peter L Galison, 'War Against the Centre', *Grey Room 4* (Cambridge, MA: MIT Press, 2001), 7–31.

in-between, begins to encumber the fantasy of overcoming. The One-Hour Commute is invented. Time and geography become one: bastard urbanism redux.

This third-generation city is no longer dominated by space, but by *time*. A post-geographical era commences.

The little-known Swedish geographer Torsten Hägerstrand eloquently pursued the union of space and time in a theory of *time–geography*. He writes:

> [Time–geography] is inspired by *notation*, which is related to the formulas of chemistry and to musical notation. Notation emphasises the bindings between base elements as in chemical formulas, and it seeks to describe configurations in space and their succession in time, in the way that musical notation describes streaming sound.[2]

The similarity of 'bindings between base elements' to the role of the in-between in suburban geography is striking. Writing about the science of the 1950s, Hägerstrand points out that when an object is taken out of its context and isolated, the forces that impinge on it in space and time are removed, and this leads to 'much loss of understanding'. Architects, developers and builders operating in suburbia have acted similarly, ignoring the very ground that makes their enterprise possible. Every project, every house, every subdivision is on its own. Time–geography attacks this limitation, by suggesting that the most central issue in the situation-sciences (geography and history) is how human beings, society, technology and nature 'engage each other in repeatedly new configurations'.[3]

2. G Carlestam and B Sollbe (eds), *Om tidens vidd och tingens ordning. Texter av Torsten Hägerstrand* (Stockholm: Byggforskningsrådet, 1991), 133. My emphasis and translation from the Swedish.

3. Ibid, 113, '*griper in i varandra i ständigt nya figurationer*' ('engaging each other in steadily new configurations').

In Houston the concentration on projects (subdivisions, malls) has led to a failure to engage the context of the entire region, best demonstrated by the sprawling of these same projects. Sprawl usurps the in-between so as to avoid potential conflicts between 'incompatible uses' (in denser cities resolved by zoning) and simultaneously ignores the overall functioning of the city. By not minding the gap, sprawl has become the solution to the development equation. This is the true libertarian ground beyond zoning, beyond government. The organisation of groups of objects, such as a cluster of subdivisions, are left to individual initiative. Hägerstrand poetically refers to this *perspectival vision* of objects in space as 'objects beyond objects', and their intricate and complex doings as 'events beyond events' (time) and we might add, in terms of society, humans beyond humans.[4] These are the kernels of a regional perspective.

In Hägerstrand's exploration of the time-dependent territory of the in-between, three domains are recognised: the *substrate*, ground or site in architectural terms or geography in my prior discussions; the *medium*, air and water; and the *populations* of humans and other physical entities (including 'stones and manufactured things such as chairs, pens and cars'). In Houston this conception takes on special meaning since our substrate is the peculiarly impenetrable gumbo-soil engraved by the foul waters of engineered bayous; and our medium of air is an ectoplasm itself: thick as liquid, and humid.

This sudden emergence of recognisable *topoi* adds time and perspective (in this case reflecting on the rise of consumer society) that give thickness to the sprawling city. Hägerstrand

4. He uses these two images to succinctly describe space: you stand next to an object and beyond that is another, and another until they disappear over the horizon, in terms of time you imagine one event behind another one, and so on.

suggests a diagram that, like a diorama, allows us to see the city in history:

First we place an observer in the middle. Outwards from the observer follow things beyond things. But these are the result of appearances (births), not all at the same time. This requires us to add an axis of time. That which appears now and at the same time may have had a varied existence.[5]

Houston has a history, speeded up by extreme urbanisation and a foreshortened time-perspective. Here the coarseness of development, its tendency to leave gaps, to jump across space unencumbered by any obstacle, allows an entire range of *topoi* to reveal the past of the city. Thus, a fragment of an African-American settlement in the Fourth Ward stands almost intact next to downtown. Tightly packed shotgun houses replete with front porches and resident population define a narrow street grid. Despite disrepair, they exude obvious efficiency and communal charm.

Packing

The historical remnant known simply as the Fourth Ward stares out at me. From 1839 until 1905, 'wards' were the city council districts of Houston. After a new system of representation was adopted in 1905, the term 'ward' continued to identify neighbourhoods within each of these former districts, especially by residents of Houston's oldest African-American neighbourhoods in the former Third, Fourth and Fifth Wards. Closely packed into a narrow grid, the Fourth Ward defies suburban principles, harkening back to the traditional city.

5. Op cit, 133.

'Material things', writes Hägerstrand, 'are thus packed vari-
ously' producing demands on the living that we more or less
willingly engage.[6] *Proxemics* (a notion developed by ET Hall[7])
or what I call 'American Distance', is predicated on socially
constructed packing. Houses sitting almost squarely in the
middle of a lot some twenty blocks from the Fourth Ward
produce a totally different 'material dependence'. The
question of material dependence – known in German as
Sachzwang, the force or influence of the thing on us – is
complicated and vague. Most of us involved with architecture
believe that the environment affects us, although we are very
leery about determinism. Thus a Fourth Ward shotgun house
in which each room must be passed through to reach the next
will have a very different effect on family life than the single-
family house with corridors serving separate rooms. The same
goes for a densely packed community served by a grid of
streets and its opposite, a subdivision with winding roads and
large lots sitting back from it. Again, we can expect a different
effect on human behaviour in each environment, but how or
what exactly is open to speculation.

In the implied interactions in these varying habitats spins
the motor of urbanisation: the interaction between humans
and things ranging from the visual to the haptic, and now
including the virtual (telecommunication) cut loose from the
physical world. Loosely packed populations (of humans and
material) depend more on actual and virtual networks than do
residents of the Fourth Ward, where the street still exists and
the front porch still functions. What happens when the ancient
street is erased and we replace face-to-face interaction with
blogs and email – when the human face is mere speculation

6. Op cit, 132.
7. *The Hidden Dimension* (Garden City,
NY: Doubleday, 1966).

and language the only test of reality? Is this the inevitable
evolution of American Distance, we have overcome isolation
for good and yet remain safely apart?

A World under Construction

We must hope the improved networks have had a huge
remedial effect on the loosely packed suburban conurbation.
Mobile phones developed as the result of a diminished
physical network – an insatiable craving for face-to-face
interaction is second-bested with ear-to-ear. Similarly,
television and later the computer have replaced the porch.
Besides material and energy, products of exchange,
information, knowledge and social interaction must be carried
and shared by individuals. This enhancement of interaction
among Hägerstrand's third category of *populations* may
suggest that the *substrate*, the first category, must be
complemented by a fourth dimension somewhat like the
second category, *medium*. When employed by populations,
these new enhancements engage all three categories
simultaneously. As he points out, a book is a mere assembly
of signs unless a human reads it. These often-virtual flows of
exchange may even include mental processes since so many
of our capabilities seem to be genetically imprinted and
therefore shared by many, if not all. Consequently, even if we
stand absolutely still in a room, our busy minds are at work
at each instant and uniquely so, since we do not have total
recall. Layering all these forces together, the world at hand
offers up an astonishing complexity that we will never fully
understand. To think of it as a static, embedded structure is
no longer possible. 'We and the world around us are under
constant construction', Hägerstrand concludes. Two worlds,

the one outside and the one in our mind, mix together and stand in relation to each other in such 'a rich way that the interactions are impossible to fully describe'.[8]

The time–geography emerging from this excursion reveals a necessity to triangulate between geography (points and lines), morphology (space and form) and metabolism (time and energy) to allow further understanding of 'the multitude of errands' performed by 'the multitude of populations' in the suburban city – millions of agents from humans to energies coursing through ethers, walls, windows, wires, elevators, tunnels, sidewalks and parking garages all on separate yet obscurely orchestrated errands. To escape this daunting complexity at least momentarily, I take direction from Herbert Blumer, a symbolic interactionist sociology teacher from my undergraduate days, who famously said in a seminar: 'When in doubt, go out and look.'[9]

Itinerary 1 (Outer Loop)

Since the everyday suburbanite commutes or otherwise makes destination trips, one must adopt the habits of a nomad to read the attenuated conurbation. Next to me in the car: historian Stephen Fox, navigator and captain. I drive a 15-year-old Ford Explorer with barely 60,000 miles on it, which suggests that long hauls are not my custom. We drive 100 miles of Houston before returning to our point of departure for fish tacos and beer. Fox remarks that despite the mileage we

8. Op cit, 141.
9. As told to me by my Berkeley colleague, sociologist W Russell Ellis. See also: Herbert Blumer, *Symbolic Interactionism: Perspective and Method* (Englewood Cliffs, NJ: Prentice-Hall, 1969).

have not in fact visited Deyan Sudjic's 100-mile city, but another form of human conurbation.[10]

For the urbanist seeking a comprehensive overview, this conurbation forms a territory with no discernible limits yet with enough internal consistency to suggest coherence. In a bizarre sense this can never really be the urbanist's territory because it is too unruly, too ungraspable. Urbanism is here permanently undermined, replaced by a nomadic, neo-Situationist or laconic curiosity that simply roams, propelled by internal combustion and turbulence rather than any destination or sense of territorial understanding.

Without leaving Houston, we have been 'everywhere' – in Portofino, a lifestyle centre (ridiculously) patterned after Venice (presumably that name was already taken), replete with a snippet of the Grand Canal and reasonable facsimile of the Doge's Palace, housing the usual franchise suspects: Old Navy, Dress Barn, Oshman's Sporting Goods, all loosely centred around a (hilarious) replica Bernini fountain. (Rome's Piazza Navona?)

We also touched down in the ultimate planned suburb, a universe orchestrated simply by forcing buyers to buy from one developer and one designer. Everything looks the same: too large, isolated and unobtrusively protected, embedded in an impenetrably dense East Texas forest broken only occasionally by golf course, artificial lake or canal.

These two distinctive 'points' are 'connected' by an endless strip more or less articulated by intensity, age and undulating linearity. Repetition – what has been called the American Highway DNA – reveals everything to really be the same. The parking apron rises from relative obscurity to become the most familiar site, thanks to ubiquity, a sort of visual muzak. We are

10. Deyan Sudjic, *The Hundred Mile City*
(Orlando, FL: Harcourt, 1993).

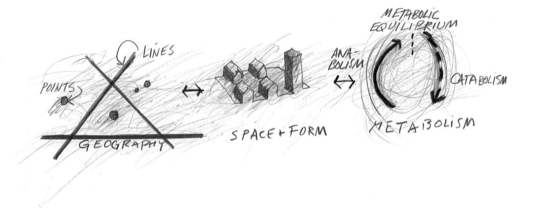

Geography / Space + Form / Metabolism

still in the same corridor, in the same speed zone, in the same territory – all on planet Sprawl. The higher up the food chain on this flat planet, the more order, the more design. At the Lifestyle Centres, the crude mass-franchise sequence is re-placed by a DNA which caters to the self and its adornments; as it were, a marketing double-helix closer to the body. At the lower end of the chain, in failed strip-malls or along partially evolved strips, new commercial mutations take shape, presum-ably with the goal of climbing higher.

In these tattered physical patterns there is a direct reflec-tion of the origins of the dispersed Southern city, as begun in Houston when the Allen Brothers built the first block of specu-lative real-estate on Main Street, in an age of less design, much less planning and more sheer speculation – an era of blunt generative energy with no time for contemplation. This north-ern plane of Houston (which we have barely touched) betrays a historical complexity from super-controlled über-design to laconic laissez-faire. Such is the nature of the libertarian outer loop in the Flatlands. The Outer Loop, roughly Harris County, is an 'open' field in which almost anything goes. Each activity is its own errand – 'an errand', to paraphrase the historian Perry Miller, 'into the *suburban* wilderness'. With this in mind, we set off in search of life forms amongst Houston's outer spokes and loops.

Itinerary II
(Going West – Actually, Southwest)

With an outdated key map on his lap, Fox takes us along Main Street. Here beyond the inner loop it is no longer a main street but just another hapless linearity lacking destination. Fox's continuous updates to the map reinforce this: changed street

72

names, added intersections, new subdivisions – driver and navigator both are explorers.

Fox reminds me of the little book that Olmstead wrote on his trip through Texas, and in particular of his comment on how messy Southerners were. Is modern messiness, still visible at the lower end of the development food chain, a continuation of history and habit? JB Jackson thought that leaving an old car wreck in the front yard was perfectly practical since any of its parts might help rescue a younger car from demise. The lower end of the attenuated settlement is the result of extreme pragmatism: all there, close enough, good enough, I know where I'm going! Since so much of suburbia is made up of development of the 'lesser kind', the general map is peppered with designed high points and planes set in a hodgepodge of in-between: the middle landscape. Navigating this irascible plane requires a type of natural GPS that every suburban driver with a purpose seems to have.

The radical discrepancy between the built and the living is not uniform, although from an urbanist perspective, behaviour and form in suburbia seem forever divorced from each other. Traditional city forms and the forms of life in them are literally synomorphic (similar in form) while most forms of interaction in suburbia are not directly traceable in its physical layout. This apparent discrepancy is clearly enhanced by the Network Society, described by Manuel Castells.[11] As a consequence, from individual perspectives there are many points on the suburban map where behaviour and form coincide – as in the case of a new Hindu temple or a typical gated community with its rules and regulations. Physical determinism – the urbanist's secret fantasy – never works without a firm (potentially

11. See Manuel Castells, 'Prologue: The Net and the Self' in *The Rise of the Network Society* (Oxford: Blackwell, 2000), 1–25.

despotic) hand holding each dweller in place. Left to their own devices people, and motorised humans in particular, shape their own itineraries and construct territoriality out of the most shapeless land masses. The odd, and in many ways wonderful thing about the outer loop is that all these roving desires can be indulged, provided one can afford it.

A map of projected freeways in the county appears at the level of points and lines as a totally irrational expression of dollars available to build freeways, with no cents left to lead them anywhere. Much like giant worms, snippets of freeway occur in strange parallel with gated communities, as their necessary appendix. It is as if the subdivision, like an insect, projects its physiology beyond its organic confinement in order to protect, for as long as possible, the migrations of its inhabitants, a notion reinforced by the fact that these snippets of freeway are in fact toll-roads built as extensions of the gated community.

The sub-centre of First Colony, a domain of sequestered subdivisions, is Sugar Land town centre.[12] As abruptly as it appears (and I can't say how Fox found it), it disappears. Backing up, I notice that it is built on an almost-grid with a

---

12. Sugar Land is located in northeast Fort Bend County, 25 miles southwest of Houston. With the exclusion of a direct relation to oil, Sugar Land is a compressed history of the evolution of the Houston Field. It dates back to a Mexican land grant awarded to Stephen F Austin, who in turn granted the land to Samuel M Williams in 1828. Known as the Oakland Plantation, the land was first planted with cotton, corn and sugar cane; a raw-sugar mill was built in 1843. Through new ownership a sugar refinery was built and a railroad. After the death of the new owners in 1864, the plantation languished. EH Cunningham then purchased 12,000 acres of the property now extending all the way to Brazos river. From 1910 until 1959, Sugar Land was a self-contained company town housing the Imperial Sugar Company. Most of the labour was leased from a nearby state prison farm and worked under horrible conditions. New owners bought the property in 1906–08. Through steady agricultural and industrial improvements the Imperial Sugar Company operated the land, the ranch and a series of mercantile interests. The last sugar cane crop was harvested in 1928. In a series of ups and downs the population held steady around 2,500. In 1946 the Kempner family became to sole owner of Sugar Land. Having expanded the company town through additional subdivisions and a series of land sales, incorporation in 1959 eventually culminated in the masterplanned First Colony of 1977, encompassing 10,000 acres. Today the population of Sugar Land is around 80,000. Adapted from Bettye J Anhaiser, 'SUGARLAND, TX', Handbook of Texas Online (http://www.tshaonline.org/handbook/online/articles/hfs10)

town square, some monumental buildings (offices and the City Hall) and along this grid actual sidewalks with directly accessible stores. But this 'city' is not even alphabetic because it's so truncated, just giving a whiff of the traditional city without fooling anyone as to where they really are. How did this facsimile of a town, some European city postcard or aborted piece of Disneyland, arrive here? The effect is totally absurd. But then again, it isn't. This is still alphabet city, its half-baked stories always interrupted by fiction and held together, indeed made rational, by motorisation.

Houston has over 3,000 registered 'churches'. Passing *La Luz del Mundo* (a church belonging to a sect of Mexican Protestants), a visiting Anglican minister from the East Coast (with whom I once shared a limousine ride) laconically noted: 'There seems to be too much religion in Houston'. Places of worship play a major role in the landscape here – the temple has replaced the plaza. One such place of worship Fox led me to while meandering through the county's southwest corner appeared suddenly as a *fata morgana* around a bend in the road. Built with 3,826 tonnes of Italian marble and Turkish limestone, the *mandir* or Hindu temple 'with its towering white pinnacles, smooth domes and glittering marble pillars'[13] juts up against the horizon of a gated community. Behind this fence, the asphalt-shingled roofs of suburban homes look particularly pathetic by comparison. The juxtaposition of suburbia's standard sticks-and-stone construction and the temple (wired with fibre optics to glow at night) built by volunteers over the course of 16 months with pre-cut stones shipped from India – itself an unsettling contrast to the *mandir*'s purported tranquillity, 'a place of paramount peace'. But such is the premise of the alphabetic city – anything goes so long as you can buy the land and

13. See: www.swaminarayan.org

75

finance construction. Whatever confusion results, the visitor must resolve.

At another bend of the road, Fox points out a subdivision – part of the masterplanned First Colony – large estates belonging to some of the more prominent members of Houston's athletic community. This type of professional striation begins to reveal the socio-cultural and economic make-up of the libertarian creed. Here a huddle of athletes, there a religious sect. Affluence allows differences to spatialise. Far beyond the traditional outliers (such as the golfing community or pet-free apartment complex), these gatherings of the like-minded are new suburban formations whose inhabitants are bound by professional or ideological solidarity.

This newly divided social landscape challenges the smooth demographics of the traditional city. Further atomisation of the suburban domain is unlikely to promote the construction of unified community – self-realisation rather than collectivity rules the day. These new formations allow an intimacy that the traditional subdivision's socio-cultural similarity lacks, because its cultural connections are weak or non-existent. Having teenage children is a less compelling commonality than being members of the same baseball team. New categories may lead to strong alphabetic (internal) conditions, but no real democratic (external) community grammar. Welcome to Stim-City.

Itinerary III (down on the bayou)

Driving through Buffalo Bayou from Barrio Segundo along the ship channel to Galveston Bay, in the southeastern section of the city, is a peculiar and troubling experience. The whole stretch from downtown to the bay is occupied by three chief activities: shipping, the refining of oil, and housing. If zoning were ever called for, it would be here. The absurdities of this literal occupation of the bayou, possibly Houston's greatest ecological asset – in fact, the purpose of the moist prairie itself – is graphically demonstrated in the few stretches of almost-natural, sinuously curving river. Weaving back and forth along and across the bayou, we are no longer in suburbia proper. But because the bayou domain is also attenuated it too is utterly pragmatic. Like the domain of the subdivision, but dominated by the petroleum industry, the bayou domain is an ad hoc and unsentimental ode to the utilitarian, somehow always subtext in the middle landscape.

Endless acres of exposed equipment for refining oil into gas and other chemical compounds are incomprehensible in their myriad pipes, cylindrical cisterns, hovering spheres, scaffolding, spigots alternatively spewing open flames or plumes of white smoke and priapic towers pointing aimlessly toward a yellowing sky. Metaphorically, this metal landscape is built of locomotives stripped of their wheels, engineers and the call to deliver men and materiel – now grounded and dedicated to the arduous task of quenching our insatiable thirst for energy. What will happen in their next transformation? Oil executives are already talking about scrapping these monstrous sites. What do they have in mind: new super-efficient, water-cooled nuclear reactors? After all, the bayou is right there – too liquid to plough, its water too viscous to drink.

Fox takes me to the end of the road, just below the huge turning basin, the end point of the ship channel (the 57-mile-long navigable river dredged in 1911 and recently widened to accommodate separate barge lanes). Across the wide water, three gigantic ships are moored stern to aft. Huge cranes are loading silently, but steadily and without interruption. Ships with the names of Energy Pioneer and Chemical Queen, flying

Liberian and Singapore flags, seem familiar to me (being of maritime stock, although the Swedes 'went ashore' many years ago) but strangely foreign to the moist prairie with its archipelago of little houses. The illegitimacy of the ships in this middle-class utopia is made clear by their clandestine presence; there seems to be no way of getting closer to them. Clearly one of the largest harbours in the world – the Houston Port Authority claims sixth place after Singapore, Shanghai, Rotterdam, Antwerp and Long Beach – it is not part of the suburban culture in the way the harbour is integral to the city in Rotterdam or in Gothenburg where, as a kid, I ran under the cranes, awestruck by stevedores struggling burdens across narrow gangplanks and huge rats scuttling over the rubber collars of mooring lines. In Houston's ship channel, perhaps owing to its artificial construction, the ships of the high sea strike one as alien.

Yet the most alien creatures along these strands of the river are forlorn housing precincts. Within some 80 miles, a dozen fragments of towns, subdivisions, and villages sit in competing states of disrepair. Barrio Segundo, El Mercado del Sol, Fifth Ward, Central Park, Port of Houston, Magnolia Park, Harrisburg, Manchester, Pasadena, Deer Park, Lynchburg, La Porte, Baytown, Shoreacres, Seabrook. Even despite a prominent past, these fragments of habitation evoke hesitation in their decline, a second thought – or simply loss of stamina. In the darkest corner of the city's toxic shadow, people of limited means stick desperately to the littoral edge of the economic and geographic bubble of suburban life.

The legitimacy of housing at the edge of the bayou is historically confirmed in every known river town of any significance, although here made absurd by hulking 'neighbours from hell'. Even the bayou becomes a mere delivery system for all forms of effluent, offal, jetsam and flotsam. What are we left with in this vast territory?

We know now that the residents along this grand waterway got a raw deal, while the oil companies have free range and maritime concerns a convenient place to load and unload goods, serviced by an army of 18-wheelers and resplendent highways – leading to the suburbs, of course. When the Jacinto Monument – memorialising the relatively uneventful battle between the Texans and Mexicans[14] – emerges at the end of a rutted street in Harrisburg (by classical design), we wonder whether it will be renamed when the bayou is won back. Because a far more glorious battle will be fought before the channel's ships are embraced by the city and the petroleum wastelands atoned for.

Forming a part of the outer perimeter of the suburban development sphere, the bayou domain is both an expression of the libertarian drive (most evident in the vast expansion of the petrochemical industry) and its side effects. Not just the effect of a toxic shadow but that of benign neglect ('as long as you don't bother us, we won't bother you'), which has allowed politically and economically weak housing precincts to form semblances of community – by accident and by necessity.

14. The Battle of Jacinto took place a month after the Texian defeat at Alamo in 1836, but this time the Texians won and sealed the fate of a new Texas.

Forensics

The first shock of Houston is unsettling: I am blinded by unfamiliarity. My previous skill at reading cities, honed in the tight fabric of European metropoles, proves useless here. There are no proper streets, no boulevards, no plazas, no fabric with quaintly inserted monuments. It takes quite a while for me to make sense of what first seemed chaos. The inadequacy of the ancient perspective with its fixed eye – the view down a street corridor with a magnificent church at its terminus – strikes me at once. In this new type of suburban city the visual field is wide and roaming, constantly changing. Cars are the movie cameras through which one constantly scans the built environment. Whoever wields the automobile must have an audio-visual memory, perceive in a filmic manner and possess the human analogues to slow motion, rewind, erasure, jump-cut, juxtaposition and fast-forward technology. Without these, suburbia is a bore.

Traditionally, shape is what distinguishes a city. But Houston's flat, seemingly endless expanse is not particularly shapely. From my high-rise perch on the 18th floor, and later through frequent roving, I discover a *relentless directionality* best observed in streets that 'cut open' the city, some better than others: Westheimer – possibly the longest city street in the world – and in parallel, Bisonette and San Felipe (homages to prominent German, French and Hispanic settlers of early Texas). Three cross streets running perpendicular: Main, Kirby and Buffalo Speedway complete a set of surgical incisions baring a city dominated by striation and direction rather than architectural form. All six have their designations as street, boulevard or avenue, and are known in name only, like shipping-lines on a vast sea. Driving on Westheimer for an hour, and sometimes two, it becomes clear that Houston has no horizon, only extent – it is *field*, in contrast to the traditional streetscape. The spread of this field in all directions is oceanic, readymade for exploration but also nausea-inducing. Even today I never really know where I am at any given moment, just that I am still here – and frequently stuck in traffic – in the doldrums of a Sargasso city.

Roving the field 'near and far' generates a dynamic – a cadence – a spatial muzak played over and over again, erratic and unpredictable yet ever present. To make sense of the world rapidly approaching through the windshield and subsequently disappearing, drivers careening down the highway perfect their skills. The undulating vistas connecting seemingly broken postage stamps of urbanisation, simplistically referred to as sprawl, require new comprehension. Motorists must become attuned not only to driving instruments and views through the windshield and rear-facing mirrors, but also to the 'rhythm' of the ride: its speed, its turns, its vibrations. This agility compensates for the vagaries experienced at great speed. Stationary bodies, diffuse patterns and occasional familiar sights take shape over time and through repetition, attaining visibility along the highway. Fleeting urban shapes are constructed, less evolved and more generic then traditional cityscapes. Suddenly they appear: first as fuzzy outlines, then as sharp figures. Despite their visual inconsistency, these large agglomerations of matter over time and repetition become, *urban facts*, large and often elastic – as if alive.[1]

New Shape

Take the driver's view of downtown Houston. Seen by a distracted navigator, shifting his gaze from roadway to

1. 'Urban fact' is an indirect reference to Aldo Rossi's work on the traditional city that has influenced most urbanists of my generation. See: *The Architecture of the City* (1966) (Cambridge, MA: MIT Press, 1984).

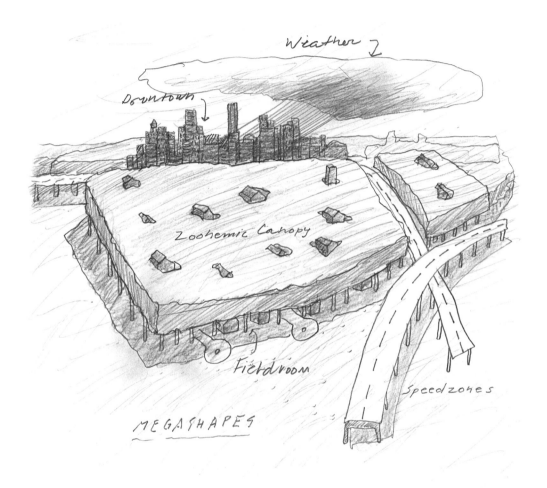

Megashapes (Fieldroom, Zoohemic Canopy, Downtown,
Speedzones and Weather)

peripheries, the aggregation of towers takes on a single, emerging form. To maintain such an evolving fullness, its appearance must be quite large and last long enough to make a driving impression. Yet downtown is also 'thick' and complex – not a Potemkin facade. Embedded in its figurative simplicity is a world often as variegated as the traditional city from which it draws inspiration. Combine a drive-by with a visit to downtown's interior configuration, and the *megashape* comes alive, revealing figure, character, atmosphere and that peculiar similarity shared by all downtown urban areas.

Constructed over time, this suburban body is not a traditional architectural object, set solidly in space, place and time, but rather a type of fleeting fiction – a *streaming* and *evolving* object shaped by the driver-perceiver. Since it is a personal, transitory experience this dense, figurative megashape is hard to corroborate and, as we shall see, harder to place. To complicate things, the downtown megashape is not the only megashape in the metropolitan field. Houston's *zoohemic canopy* (an urban forest of trees of varying species, size and maturity, that together with the flat ground plane forms a potentially 'enchanted suburban forest' that I call the *fieldroom*) is so dominant that it too is a type of megashape. Similarly it is the vast desert and its peculiar arroyos, aridity, daily heat sinks and nightly chill, forming a hard floor that dominates everything and everyone in Phoenix. The polder-scape constructs and brackets Randstad in Holland, while an invasive industrial infrastructure takes hold of Germany's Ruhrgebiet. Although diffuse, these megashapes come to characterise entire cities and regions. Yet the canopy of trees in Houston has no horizon, and the desert only an imaginary one; their shapeliness stems from repetitive interiority, from sheer persistence. Their extent and overall shape – the edge of the forest or the desert – are fictional.

Fieldroom (Reconstituted Moist Prairie)

By contrast, downtown, powerfully present from all directions, relies on its dramatic figure and various striations, both in plan and elevation. The common denominator of this spectrum of megashapes is internal consistency, achieved through repetition of a multitude of near-identical elements: fully mature trees and high-rise buildings or totalising ecological conditions or geological similarity. The juxtaposition of dense figures and diffuse agglomerations of similarity and repetition give distinctive individuality to each of these middle landscapes.

Though dense and diffuse megashapes are different, both become visible through shifting positions and distortions of scale and speed during repeat encounters. When approached by car, downtown, which is perceived as one great shape, relies less on speed than on distance. Once inside, unitary perception is flooded with diverse complexity. As such, downtown emerges as a fully fledged entity over time, rich in content, with its own shape and striation; while the 'endless' fieldroom shaped by the canopy (a megashape also present in Arizona's desert floor and Dutch polders) requires a special attentiveness since it operates at the periphery of everyday encounters. Moving at the fringes of the distracted driver's attention, trees, desert sand, bodies and channels of running water eventually 'get counted',[2] or are 'appreciated' with time and familiarity – even pedestrians get a sense of the middle landscape. Since field-, desert- or polder-room is understood from within, its spaciousness evolves between the ground and the underside of its 'ceiling' – be it the zoohemic canopy or the sky, darkly blue and hazy grey – every suburbanite's 'living room', whether in Houston, Phoenix or Utrecht. Although a diffuse megashape must be imagined and constructed in the

2. As Henry Glassie performed for *Folk Housing in Middle Virginia* (Knoxville, TN: University of Tennessee Press, 1975), 'counting' is a form of sophisticated anthropological mathematics that would serve us well here – if we had the time, patience, resources.

mind of its denizens, the pillared roominess of the zoohemic canopy in Houston (like the etchings of Piranesi's *carceri)* promises a 'beyond'. In Phoenix the dryness and sand chirping underfoot presages endless desert, whereas the constant threat of water to the polder constructs, time and again, a vast specificity. Each of these ecological characteristics gives the city a unique aura, undermining any description of it as 'mere sprawl'.

But such fundamentals fade in everyday life, since most suburban locations are always under construction by their residents, who leave behind the old city, its multitude and manifest presence – resulting in a semi-private conception that may be more of a fiction than an actually verifiable presence. In the diffuse city, reaching a destination relies on maps and signs, rarely on physical description, unless referring to a distinct figure, such as the occasional dense megashape whose shapeliness – historically the city's distinguishing feature – stands in stark contrast to its shapeless setting. Once in focus, there are at least two ways to apprehend it: from the inside, leading to an appreciation of the algorithm of its shape (or *taxis);* and from the outside, leading to an understanding of the whole (its *figure).* From the road, these megashapes – no longer quite grounded – grow footloose as billiard balls. 'Is the shopping centre down this street, or the one I just passed?', wonders the equally footloose populace operating in distracted search-mode.

Aside from this combination of projective and extensive megashapes that forms the ground zero of my investigation, there are of course other shapes in the diffuse middle land-scape: the mile-long row of cars in a traffic jam, the partially orchestrated swarm of football players, the subdivision of houses. Unfortunately, these 'externalities' will regularly mud-dle our work, creating a multitude of other objects (fixed and

89

ambulatory), atmospheres, weathers and conditions with which to contend.

Stim and Dross:
The Activity Surface

Taken as a living surface, the vast plane of Houston becomes an undulating topography, raised by peaks of activity and elsewhere simultaneously flattened to a halt. On an 'activity surface', dynamism and quiet co-exist. *Stim*, as in stimulation and *dross*, as in mere residue, are catalysed by a mixture of human movement, communication, noise and action. The constant 24/7 activity block of the traditional centric city does not exist in the tattered fabric of the middle landscape. Never really contiguous, the activity of the day-and-night lifecycle is interrupted by lulls, interruptions, skips and hops. Times and spaces where the activity cloak gapes in underlying stillness reveal the mysterious abyss of nature. We rely on the opposite of dross to disguise this dark abyss: stim combats isolation, boredom, loneliness and despair. But compared to the lively and ongoing cycle of the old city, sustained stim is a scarce commodity here. Stim and dross – as if setting alternating patterns of sound and silence to score an oft-disrupted geography – characterise the middle landscape.

Stim is generally orchestrated and confined to space or location, never spontaneous but occasionally accidental. Normally associated with mobility, it is heightened here to frenzy, pressure, drive. 'We must have fun' or 'we must work hard'. To modulate stim, dross becomes a necessity, even a commodity. One cannot exist without the other. These two vectors animate and slow the activity surface. In the mind's eye, this surface comes alive like a giant ectoplasm – one

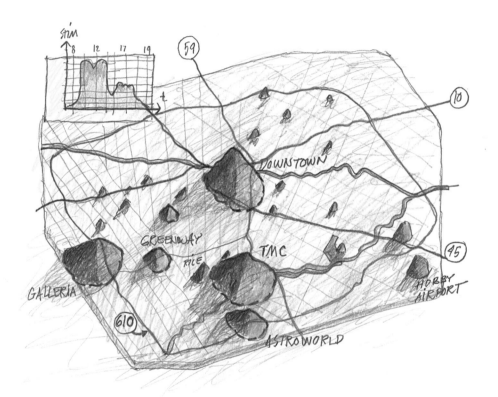

Activity Surface

Stim and Dross

begins to view it as a designable surface – an expansive architectural ground to which we can add or from which we can take away. Evolved and quantified, the activity surface becomes the new ground – ground that is no longer cast in concrete as the plazas and boulevards of the traditional city, but as a living substance with elastic metrics open to incentives, speculation, demise, revival. Boom and bust, *Sturm und Drang*.

Holey Plane

Drive southwest on Main through Houston's almost booming downtown, expectant midtown and then out along South Main and you will experience the volatility of the suburban real-estate drama. Here the priapic heights of skyscrapers tumble down into blocks of stolid commercial boxes, occasionally enlivened by peculiarities such as Isabella Court (a dream of an apartment house that could have been a model for the entire city, but instead remains a melancholy reminder of lost intelligence) sections of the Metro light rail and clusters of restaurants associated with tram stops (location, location, location), until finding new enthusiasm in and around Texas Medical Center, only to fade and break into bursts of activity in the giant Astro domain, its dome once a Wonder of the World. Under its skull cap 'the subconscious of the freeway mind' could play out its wildest dreams in stock car races, demolition derbys and monster truck Meets, however now abandoned for an *adjacent* new stadium designed for sports even more attuned to Middle America – football, rodeos, ballroom dancing. Otherwise, South Main lies dormant, barely aboriginal in light of its illustrious beginnings in downtown.[3]

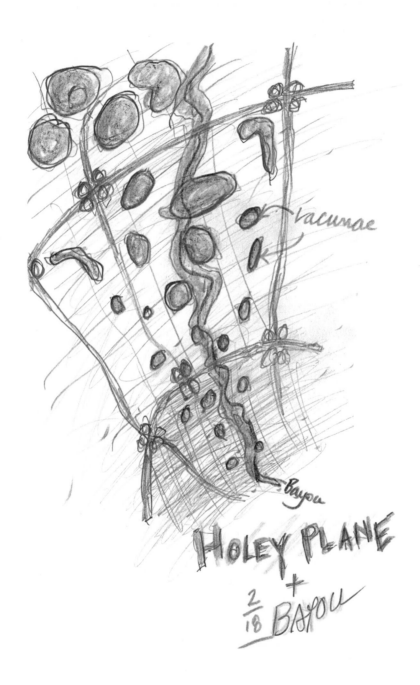

The Holey Plane

Scrutinising this section through the activity surface reveals a pattern of long-term lulls and breaks that reflect a fundamental aspect of American development. The vast amount of space open to urbanisation combined with the availability of transportation collude to produce an attenuated city – a built fabric stretched frequently to breaking points that remain undeveloped, often for decades. In fact, it is business as usual: the peculiar mixture of real-estate economics – the ready availability of financing – and this open plane have allowed developers to seek and find the best land-deal at a particular place and time. This has led to so-called 'leapfrogging' in which more expensive land is skipped over to reach cheaper land a bit further out. It is a steeplechase across urbanising land that leaves the losers behind and propels the winners ahead. These holes in developed land, somewhere between the determined and the chaotic, make for a seemingly haphazard city. Yet they hold promise: savvy developers grab them for future development when the price is right.

Fits and starts are integral to mobility. Leapfrogging is its most graphic expression and the ragged gaps between subdivisions, more than occupied space, hold in their dicey future a true terra incognita. They may well be breathing holes essential to a fabric threatened by total development and privatisation. Here the moist prairie lives in the raw, a complex ecology that may hold the key to the future of the subdivided middle landscape.

3. In writing this I suddenly realise that I have omitted the newly constructed tramline coursing down the centre of Main and connecting downtown with the Astro domain. Public transportation, with its elongated beads of stops, is foreign to the diffuse city; and in the end the tram remains so. In the dense city each transit stop produces real-estate activity, but not here – or not yet. Although used, the tram remains a suburban enigma that, like the miniature train in the adjacent park, amuses children while allowing parents a respite. Here the tram delights city-buffs and stirs a sense of political correctness, but has done little to decrease automobile traffic while probably shifting only former bus travellers to rail.

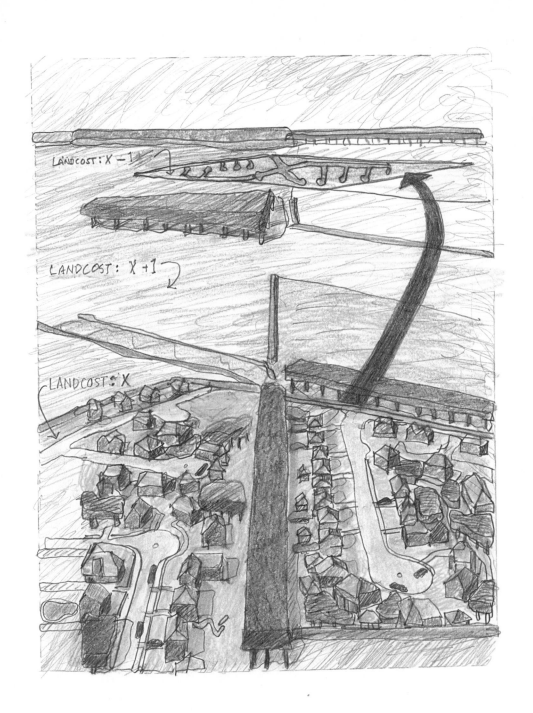

LANDCOST: X - 1

LANDCOST: X + 1

LANDCOST: X

Leapfrogging

American Distance

Shifting our attention from these gaps to the developed area itself, there is a noticeable echo of the holey plane in actual distances between buildings. It is peculiarly American.

In the summer of 1919, Lt Col Dwight D Eisenhower joined a United States Army convoy on a mission to overcome continental distance, to prepare for the construction of a system of transcontinental transportation that would join the two coasts. The origin of this deliberate drive lay not only in military mobilisation but more speculatively, I would suggest, in a nomadic urge. As successor to two previous cross-country drives, first the wagon trails, then the railroads, highways would become the choice mode of travel for individual Americans. In this sense, despite its military nature, the 1919 convoy signalled the beginnings of the self-mobilisation that 30 years later, still under Eisenhower's purview, would launch the immense American Highway Project, whose significance cannot be underestimated.

As Eisenhower suggested in his 1967 book *At Ease: Stories I Tell to Friends*, nothing on the scale of that first transcontinental convoy had been previously undertaken: to travel 3,200 miles in some 60 days from Washington, DC to San Francisco. Despite its philosophical link to American westward migration, the convoy was a military exercise rather than a private enterprise, which may explain the precision, efficiency and unquestioned purpose that still characterises the building of highways today. While the nomadic (or migrant) vector did not play a role in road construction itself, it soon found fulfilment in the private car – the fruit of Fordism – and the highway thus served a double purpose: as an untested military network in case of foreign invasion and as an actual civilian network. The astonishing proliferation of surfaced roads, combined with the mass production of motor vehicles that occurred between 1911, and today form the philosophical ground of the American suburb – the *modus vivendi* for the planet of mobility: 'I drive, therefore I think.'[4]

Here the road replaces the city, the house supplants the block, and a highly mobile community rather than a local pedestrian community is the norm: 'mobilisation replaces labour as the basic category of historical anthropology'.[5] And mobility achieves its own allure: at the end of all those tantalising highways lies a promise of freedom – the bright side of this demanding algorithm. The ability to move oneself, self-realisation, allows the individual to break away from the flock (the extended family) to join the larger community and to escape from toil itself so as to exploit its attendant surpluses. This allows individuals to create their own lives, to defy their origins and destined ends. Speed is key to the new state of nomadic being.

At this contradictory nexus of individual freedom and societal cohesion, or common good, a certain distance is born: the 'American distance'. Eisenhower's desire to overcome distance is set against an older desire to create distance. For a very long time to come American mobility will be hampered by these opposing desires, now deeply embedded in suburbanisation.

Not far behind this twin urge comes technology – the ally of American distance. Whether fictional (as in my childhood adventures influenced by German writer Karl May, whose hero, Old Shatterhand, is elaborately connected to his horse via saddle, stirrup and barely perceptible trail) or actual (in the

---

4. There are of course numerous other factors, such as massive electrification projects and streamlined steel, rubber and asphalt production, which contributed to the formation of the suburb.

5. Peter Sloterdijk, 'Modernity as Mobilisation' in Jeremy Millar and Michiel Schwarz (eds), *Speed: Visions of an Accelerated Age* (London: The Photographer's Gallery and the Trustees of the Whitechapel Art Gallery, 1998), 49.

assembly of train and railway track, or the highway and its vehicles), technology facilitates the American need for mobility. Yet the formidable assembly of traveller, vehicle and highway are of little economic value without a destination (or credit card). Here the Jeffersonian grid supplies a partial answer: tracing patterns from the Mississippi River to the coasts, the territorial bounds made the wilderness comprehensible, compartmentalised and ready for Hamiltonian commerce. This grid, etched into landscape and deed, forms the conceptual fundament – the geolegal degree zero more neutral and reliable in its simple artificiality than the reckless wilderness it held in place. Around this geometrical infrastructure, the story of American distance was begun.

Technology rather than architecture, transport rather than housing, and eventually middle landscape rather than traditional city, are the primary foci for the story of distance. The attenuated city has become an exquisite manifestation of the end of the road, a sublime coming together of software and hardware that meshes financing, mortgages, transportation, 'community' and lifestyle.

The unforeseen consequences of the gross accumulation of technology that now plagues the United States began, just like distance, with that first clear-cut in the primordial forest. Once we see it as a method or a system rather than a primary event, this first clearing proves to be the origin of the grid, the property lot and mobility itself. The clearing of the wilderness, the simultaneous destruction of nature and introduction of light and civilisation, is the principle that underlies suburban development. Out in the forest, far from the city plazas and public throngs, the individual (and individual family) embarks on that unique American journey.

The emphasis on distance and mobility avoids the merely ideological. 'True mobility' and 'overcoming distance'

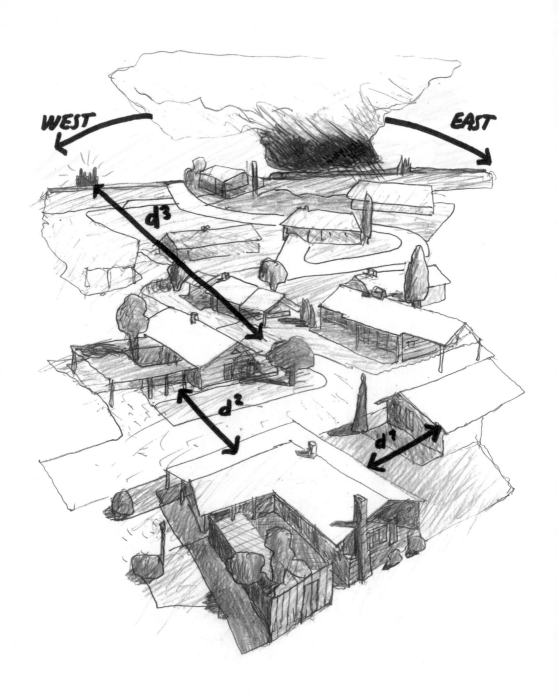

American Distance

comprise fundamental positives that enlighten all modern life, while 'mindless mobility' and the 'making of distance' may have disastrous effects. A balance is difficult to strike between the reasonable and truly liberating on the one hand, and frivolity and paranoia on the other. Only pragmatics and necessity will come to the rescue – the cry for so-called sustainability is just beginning. In the meantime, the peculiar dynamic between making and overcoming has resulted in a distinctive kinetics that shapes American lives. Mobility may have become our addiction, and concomitant separation our respite.

The holey plane is repeatedly echoed in the gaps between houses in the typical Houston subdivision. This charged separation between neighbours, between 'them' and 'us', the tension between Eisenhower's conquest of space and the Puritans' use of it as a protective barrier heats up. No longer as history, but as grammar or a suburban genetics. In the traditional plaiting of Houston subdivisions, 'making distance' seems to dominate. After all, we are in Texas: lots must be sized to Texas proportions, protected for decades by deed restrictions. But this grammar is today being challenged by baby boomers leaving the outer suburbs for the inner loop. The lacunae are disappearing as new medium-density apartment blocks shape entire sections of the city into something no longer Texan, but metropolitan. In the denser agglomerations of single-family houses, distance becomes asymptotic; a miniscule distance is preferred to a common wall. The gap remains as a microcosm, a symbolic reminder of the American expanse – the wilderness. In Houston what is left of the ancient prairie is sublimated between houses, between subdivisions, and eventually, between one city and another.

Alphabet City

Flying in from the east to land at Bush Intercontinental Airport, a generous handful of building types rush by as confetti after a giant wedding, as well as patches of dense forest, lacunae, half-finished subdivisions (after all, this is the city's edge), hangars, airplanes and tarmacs of cars and trucks arranged in the latest colours. Here American distance has another radical effect: all suburban objects are both clearly separated in their functional assemblies and yet tossed reluctantly together, at random, across the field.

Traditional readings of the city depend on perceiving morphological units, but in Houston urban figures dominate. From this result figurative *differences* such as plazas, boulevards and parks and *contiguity,* usually in the form of perimeter blocks built around a gridiron of streets, while individual uses are embedded in these larger figures. In the middle landscape, apprehension is reversed. Here we have no trouble finding the gas station, the franchise restaurant, the office building and of course the house, whereas figures on the scale of the megashape are more difficult to discern. Their reading relies on speed, focus and peripheral vision.

Lived suburban shape on the holey plane is always broken into jump cuts or deliberate blind spots that rely on selective disregard or rapid perceptual construction. The result is a substantial alphabet soup. This irregular patterning promotes a sense that the diffuse settlement is mere sprawl, yet when seen from above (a typical experience for many travellers) a stark geometry appears – stunning in its abstract simplicity. It is hard to reconcile the clarity of the view from above with the confused experience on the street below.

Shorthand metropolitan geography privileges one body and one pattern: the freeway and the subdivision. These two

Alphabet City

essential shapes, one an elongated body strung together in loose networks and the other a relentless pattern, form a crude facsimile of the vast city. However, this simplicity is deceptive since an *ambulatory grammar* has evolved. Mobility introduces new complexity: the elaborate nesting of bodies, markets, institutions, regions and economies becomes possible through motorisation and various forms of long-distance communication.

Once the traditional perimeter block with its fusion of building and street loses its typological monopoly on the architecture of the city, everything changes. Architecture is reduced to an archipelago of pavilions. Streets are freed from their dependency on, and definition by, surrounding buildings and are reduced to points of access. Over tim, by peculiar coincidence or by necessity, the loss of physical connectivity, has been replaced by a huge and highly interactive software 'city'. And while each alphabetic configuration remains discrete, external connections are increasingly ephemeral despite the underlying and partially hidden physicality of electrical grids, roads, freeway- and sewage-networks. The soft city will prosper only as long as energy is affordable, until we reach the end of the 'petroleum interval' – the era that has allowed both 'the coming together' and, more importantly, 'the keeping apart'. After this the alphabetic condition will require a new grammar dominated by coming together. Being apart will be too expensive, if not technologically impossible.

New Community

Alphabet city spreads out before us. Each building glows in supreme solitude. The metrics are clear: everything is measurable, pure geography. But how do we occupy this

104

broken fabric? Are neighbours four feet away 'closer' than those 40 feet away? How is our social world constructed?

We navigate it, we learn how to cope, how to read and to ride it. But how do we live in it? Individually we are reduced to navigators, drifting along the highways, roads and cul-de-sacs. But how do we live together and shape community in this dispersed landscape? The issue of community in alphabet city may be the most complex and disputed question concerning suburban life.

Controversy arose in 1963 with the simultaneous appearance of two publications that responded to the 1960s urban crisis from different perspectives. *Community and Privacy: Toward a New Architecture of Humanism,* by Serge Chermayeff of Yale University and Christopher Alexander of the University of California at Berkeley, was a response from within the discipline of architecture.[6] Meanwhile, Melvin M Webber, who also taught at UC Berkeley, but in a different department, published an article titled 'Order in Diversity: Community without Propinquity', which articulated the response of city planning to the same crisis.[7]

It is hard to conceive of two more different perspectives. Webber's paper proposes change based on what was found in his own research, while Chermayeff and Alexander's book advocated change based on what they wanted the world to be. Webber returned to his utterly unsentimental findings five years later in a *Daedalus* article discussing the Watts riots, in which he concludes: 'the age of the city seems to be at an end'.[8] The architects Chermayeff and Alexander beg to differ, suggesting instead that if we were to live closer together in our cities (with less noise, more traffic separation and more

6. Serge Chermayeff and Christopher Alexander, *Community and Privacy: Toward a New Architecture of Humanism* (New York: Doubleday, 1965).

7. Melvin M Webber, 'Order in Diversity: Community without Propinquity' in Lowdon Wingo (ed), *Cities and Space* (Baltimore, MD: Johns Hopkins University Press, 1963).

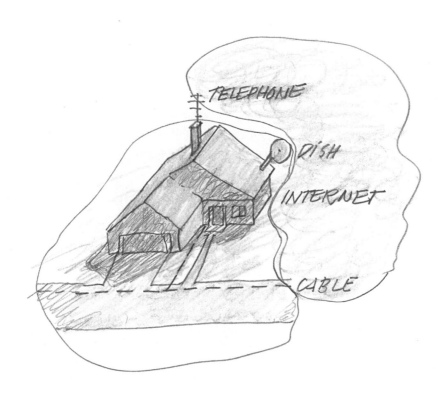

Double-space

efficient garbage collection), we would have real community and fewer social problems.[9] Webber counters that place no longer matters in the frictionless expanse of this new society:

> In the novel society now emerging – with its sophisticated and rapidly advancing science and technology, its complex social organisation and its internally integrated societal processes – the influence and significance of geographic distance and geographic place are declining rapidly. This is, of course, a most remarkable change. Throughout virtually all of human history, social organisation coincided with spatial organisation. Social communities, economies and politics were structured about the place in which interaction was least constrained by the frictions of space.[10]

The car speeding down the highway on its rubber tyres is a glorious manifestation of the frictionless. It is no wonder that a nation in the throes of constant migration, bound by centuries of cumbersome distance and serious spatial frictions, would be so enthralled by the sheer overcoming of both. This desire for mobility may very well be the most succinct way to describe the American experience. Stubbornly and aggressively idealistic, the Europeans Chermayeff and Alexander argue that all the enthusiasm for speed and dispersion is sheer nonsense in comparison to the longer history of civilisation's close

8. Melvin M Webber, 'The Post-City Age', in *Daedalus: Journal of the American Academy of Arts and Sciences* (Fall 1968): 1092–93. The quoted line is drawn from Don Martindale's introduction to Max Weber's *The City* (1962).

9. It is ironic and even sad that 40 years later architects like myself have finally discovered the significance of 'community without propinquity' and followed after Webber to declare the city passé. See my most recent book, *After the City* (Cambridge, MA: MIT Press, 2000).

10. Webber, 'Post-City Age', 1094. I do think Webber underestimated the actual value of added distance, which *increased* the importance of geographical distance – while the ease of traversing distance made possible by the car and the federal highway programmes that contributed to the city's dispersion have essentially been forgotten, their influence very much remains.

encounters (as manifested in Italian hill towns and North African souks). They propose to solve all problems by creating a single dense community based on architectural precedents. A rhetorical tour de force that quotes freely from President Kennedy, Erich Fromm, Aldous Huxley, Walter Gropius, Peter Brian Medawar, Francis Bacon, Patrick Geddes and other Western political, cultural and philosophical notables, *Community and Privacy* lays out a prevalent vision of how urban life should be lived and conducted. This proposition is purely utopian, lacking an understanding of what makes suburbanites tick: the ever-present American distance! Not even the New Urbanists (who share similar sentiments with Alexander et al) and their dreams of walking communities have abandoned this peculiar penchant for distance-making. The immense conceptual power that suburbia holds over us is not some romantic version of the Puritan organism, but a low-density pattern predicted by Webber when he wrote that the new city would spread: 'over far more extensive areas than even the most frightened future-mongers have yet predicted'.[11]

Webber correctly foretold the resulting change in community patterns that is all too obvious today. What the 'frightened future-mongers' may have sensed, if not fully articulated, was that a new type of city would result from astonishing 'technological improvements' combined with the radical expansion of the middle-class family. At the centre of this controversy lies the discrepancy between an actually performed community and ideal community. But social community did not disappear; rather it operated along a variety of new channels, including new forms of transportation (cars) and communication (telephone and internet). In fact, one could argue that this new form of community is better than the old since it no longer imposes spatial determinants

11. Ibid, 1098.

on its participants. It is voluntarily constructed: a willed community. The traditional city is no longer the organising framework of metropolitan society. Yet the direct application of Webber's 'community without propinquity' is inadequate, too, since it is entirely rooted in a frictionless physical environment. Suburban congestion has seen to that. Perplexingly, the modern metropolitan community is *virtually* near and *physically* far, outfitted with various modes of assembly – conference calls, video sharing, photo communication, virtual town meetings, local television exchange – yet without propinquity. In this new reticulum hides a measure of freedom that its progenitor Thomas Jefferson could not have imagined, especially since it opens a Pandora's box of curious contradictions.

Although the will to community is set free from spatial constraints, it may aspire to the *organic community* once set forth by the Puritans. Here the nomadic is also tribal. Thus, in the middle landscape the nomadic urge may no longer be just for the joyride but for a destination as well – be it the villages of the New Urbanists or the faith-based or the gated communities of singles, golfers, retirees. Community and privacy, the view from the end of the cul-de-sac, returns with a vengeance as the nomadic desire to roam freely turns in on itself. 'Off the grid', yes, but also off the larger community, away from society. (The Federalist's dream, perhaps?) It is hardly surprising that in the outer reaches of suburban culture this new form of 'tribal nomadism' has inverted the search for freedom – for the frontier – in favour of close belonging. This changes the tenets of American distance. Finally the vast territory is overcome, the drive to 'Go West' sublimated, reduced to virtual distance-making only; by fencing in the gates, the tribes, the new religiosity. Flocks of suburbanites dissolve into elective communities and so too the American

Dream. Now: 'My Dream'. But as always there is no tranquillity, everything is forced to move along. Yesterday's sublimation is shattered by sudden economic collapse. All gates are broken in the face of a common threat. As of this writing, dreams are a complete enigma. Today the middle landscape is at the centre of this unknown – not only toxic environmentally, but economically and mentally as well. Shopping carts have stopped rolling, while the banks hoard their savings.

The evolution of the new metropolitan community is thus a complicated tale, in which the opposing positions discussed above converge. Technology (telecommunications, cars, roads) and social surplus allow a large segment of the middle class to build its own network, but no longer in splendid physical isolation. Lacunae are beginning to fill in; the holey plane is contracting. With increased proximity, economic and social chasms fuel *derivative fear* (second-hand fear) – which is spread through media but not (yet) manifest.[12] Yesterday's virtual masked men have been replaced by mild-mannered Ponzi-scheme conmen flickering on TV screens. Paranoia is unabated. An intense desire for security continues to dominate life, but its focal point has shifted from the fence to what might be safely hidden 'under the mattress'. This fosters deep suspicion, not only of regulation, but of regulators from city hall, the American congress and other branches of government. And the original urge for mobility grows more complicated. Webber's 'friction cost' (the cost mounting with increasing distance and traffic) has taken new and unforeseen turns.

Some metropolitans share the giddiness felt by early suburban pioneers at the thought of being liberated from city shackles, believing that the centrifugal forces would never

12. Although this is rapidly changing, too.
See Zygmunt Bauman's *Liquid Fear* (Cambridge:
Polity Press, 2006), 3.

cease. Mobility and communication, the essence of globalisation, will eventually overcome friction and space will become totally irrelevant! Yet many think otherwise. Keith (Pinkie) Jackson, a maverick Houston land planner, once quipped: 'Sometimes cities breathe out, sometimes in'.[13] The recent 'breathing in' towards the inner loops, and towards scatterings of willed (and gated) communities, suggests the hydraulics of the new city can accomplish both at the same time.

But the metropolitan region impinges on suburban conventions. Middle-class communities – traditionally meaning white middle-class – still construct and conduct themselves much as Webber described, although socio-economic determinants are slowly replacing once ethnic divisions. Traditionally, African-Americans inhabited Houston's Wards, while the Hispanic population settled along Navigation Avenue just south of downtown. All this is changing. Yet the basic equation of distance and proximity seductively remains, forcing everyone, regardless of class or creed, to roam the middle landscape.

Mathematics

Coursing along the activity surface, straddling distance across the alphabetic field, leaping over walls and gates, weaving through the subdivision, we arrive at the house, or as it is referred to with affection and pride, the *home*. The meridian of the suburban world.

The typical single-family house is the fulcrum through which society and community are channelled. Distances proliferate here – between parents and children, between

13. In conversation with John Mixon, a land use lawyer in Houston.

voters and politicians, between individuals and society, between *their house* and *your home*. These are the remains of American distance – the desire to both overcome and create distance.

Down the offramp, along the frontage road and through a sharp turn, we enter the manicured subdivision. We wind along the stretches and curves, all the while counting the houses that mark their positions like numbers on a clock. The distance between houses lays the ground for the prevailing calculus, while the stretches and curves are overcome by car. Distance is everywhere – between house and street, house and neighbouring house, front and backyards. The meandering road system, with its twists and turns, closely follows the geometrical constraints of a moving car. (Besides the entry door and its walkway, all traces of pedestrian activity are absent.) Centred on its postage-stamp lot, the house sits back from the road, this distance bridged by a wide tarmac of asphalt necessary to park the car. Open space is utterly privatised in the form of front-, side- and backyards. Even in the densest subdivision, distance between houses remains. Everything is separate.

Historically, lot-size has increased over time and the sizes of houses have grown, while families have become smaller. Consequently, the density of the zoohemic canopy has decreased and the ratio of paved areas to gardens has increased, as have rates of flooding. The applied calculus of the appropriately named 'subdivision' is prefigured by the numerology of the neo-classical house, its vertical and horizontal tripartite divisions and ever-predictable internal matrix: garage, hallway, living room, dining room, kitchen, bedroom, bathroom. Thus the vortices of the 'stretches and curves' are kept in check by the striated mathematics of its component parts. In other words, the leisurely curving streets

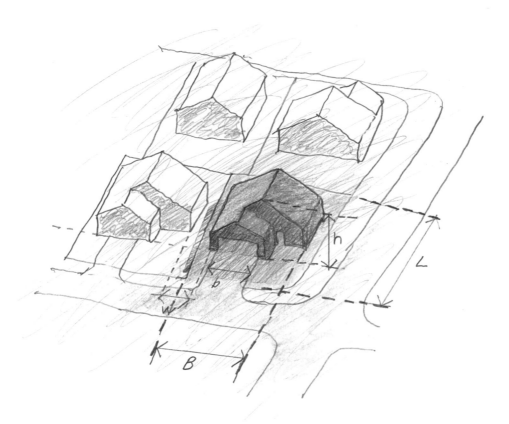

Mathematics (of the Suburban Villa)

ending in cul-de-sacs, and vaguely suggesting the presence
of nature in their smoothness, are held in place by the
strict arithmetic of real-estate practice, community regulations
such as deed restrictions and a fanatical commitment
to the numerology of the neo-classical single-family house.

But other calculations lurk behind this visibility. Take
the added distance to the shopping centre resulting from
the leapfrogging that determined the site of a particular
development. Or the equation that allowed the lowest
bidder to receive the construction contract. Or the federal
highway funds that led county planners to locate the freeway
'five minutes from our subdivision'. Luck and chance also
play a role in each cluster of calculations (and outcomes)
in the continuously transforming middle landscape.

Mathematics display, hold and hide the complexities
of suburban life – its quotidian realities and unforeseen
consequences. The ability of this mathematics to display
(and to be read) allowed Lewis Mumford to write a succinct
and convincing critique – in my view, unequalled by any
of the modern critics of sprawl – in 1961, just 10 years after
the emergence of suburbia in the nation:

> [Suburbia is] so enchanting that those who contrived it
> failed to see the fatal penalty attached to it – the penalty
> of popularity, the fatal inundation of a mass movement
> whose very numbers would wipe out the goods each
> individual sought for his own domestic circle and, worse,
> replace them with a life that was not even a cheap
> counterfeit, but rather the grim antithesis… a multitude
> of uniform, unidentifiable houses, lined up inflexibly, at
> uniform distances, on uniform roads, in a treeless
> communal waste, inhabited by people of the same class,
> the same income, the same age group, witnessing the

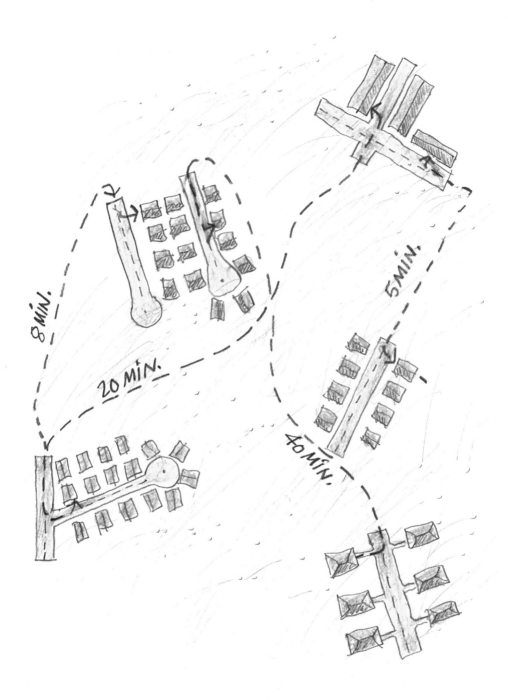

Community without Proximity

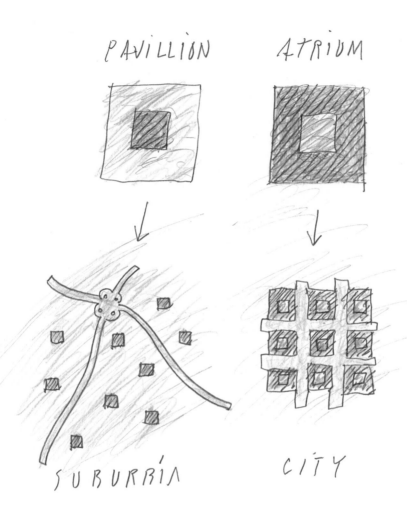

Pavilion / Suburb and Atrium / City

same television performances, eating the same tasteless prefabricated foods, from the same freezers, conforming in every outward and inward respect to a common mould, manufactured in the central metropolis … a low-grade uniform environment from which escape is impossible.[14]

Morphology

Despite the prevailing virtuality and more or less visible mathematics, the morphology of the alphabetic city is still a subject of considerable importance, not entirely exhausted by previous discussions of 'alphabetics' or 'new shape'. And although the single-family house holds everything in place and at a particular distance, its three-dimensional form enveloped in open space, combined with a magnetic symbolism, makes it the most fundamental component of the suburban city. Supremely solitary, the single-family house carries the burden and the glory of suburban culture. As *ur*-form, the 'pavilion' dominates the built morphology of the middle landscape and when assembled into a subdivision, is emblematic of the American dream.

When Sir Leslie Martin and Lionel March at The Centre for Land Use and Built Form Studies (now the Martin Centre for Architectural and Urban Studies) at Cambridge University calculated the geometric difference between the *pavilion* and *atrium* typologies (using Froebel's proposed quantitative, qualitative and relational mathematics) they demonstrated the fundamental morphological motors of the suburb and the city. By surrounding itself in a blanket of open space, the pavilion is permanently dissociated from the responsibility

14. Lewis Mumford, *The City in History* (London: Penguin Books, 1961), 553.

to construct the city – the street is free to roam. The atrium, when applied in the traditional city, forms entire blocks of apartments surrounding an inner courtyard. In turn these blocks define a gridiron of streets. Each entryway descends to the sidewalk. The street is the centre of public life, and the insertion of the natural is deliberate but incidental. In the suburbs, pavilions – single-family houses surrounded by gardens – are no longer directly attached to the street system or to each other and have lost their function as the architecture of the city. Houses are at best *examples* of architecture, certainly with individual significance but none as a manifestation of the collective. In the suburb the city loses its grip on the individual; home has replaced city as symbol of habitation. In the suburban city, nature, paradoxically unnoticed, dominates habitation.

The profound difference between the pavilion and atrium is best appreciated *in situ*. Henri Lefebvre describes the latter end of the morphological arc when he writes:

> The urban is defined as the place where people walk around, find themselves standing before and inside piles of objects, experience the intertwining of the threads of activities until they become unrecognisable, entangle situations in such a way that they engender unexpected situations. The definition of this space contains a null vector (virtually); the cancellation of distance haunts the occupants of urban space.[15]

By rephrasing Lefebvre, we see a suburban space based on the pavilion emerge:

15. Henri Lefebvre, *The Urban Revolution*, trans Robert Bonanno (Minneapolis, MN: University of Minnesota Press, 2003), 39.

Suburbia is defined as the domain where people drive around, find themselves standing before and inside singular objects, experience an activity entirely familiar, engage situations in such a way that they engender predictable situations. The definition of this space contains a cacophony of vectors; attenuated distances haunt the occupants of suburban space.

Atrium space is experienced as interior space, always surrounded by buildings, while pavilion space is experienced as exterior space. The pavilion and the atrium constitute a case study in simple topology. Topological space is at first and foremost self-similar. In the classic example, a doughnut and a cup are deemed alike since both have one hole, but profoundly dissimilar to a figure eight which has two holes (or a pavilion, a solid lump of material with no hole).

The topological litmus test serves us well in distinguishing between urban and suburban – that is, until the skyscraper appears. An American invention, the first of these sprung up on the perimeter block in Chicago. Over time it has migrated from its genealogy as a cog in the perimeter block towards something of its own morphological inclination. Unlike its prototype, the suburban skyscraper today sits on a podium of parking surrounded by 'open space'. Topologically, the high-rise building takes its proper place as a solitary pavilion.

The plot thickens once several towers are brought together (as is often the case in an 'urbanised' area of a metropolis) and the podium becomes a public realm. However, this interiorisation of public space does not replace the sidewalks of the perimeter block. In fact, it reinforces the 'solidity' of the type. The podium and its giant 'open plan' absorb the public realm to create a peculiar experiential hybrid with both suburban and urban qualities. But deceptively so, since the

Morphology

urban aspect of the podium is clearly bracketed by the form of tower and reinforced in its 'uniqueness' as a privately owned, quasi-public realm. (Closed at night, it is policed by security guards rather than city police.) Morphologically, a gaggle of towers is still a subdivision of solitary pavilions, vertical cul-de-sacs. Here in the most urban quarters of the metropolis the pavilion still rules. Can we now surmise that all suburban morphology is in the same topological family as the pavilion?

Clearly the shopping centre, the gas station and the pharmacy are, but how about the strip mall, particularly when it occupies a street corner and appears half-atrium, or the row house? From the topological litmus test, it is apparent that the L-strip is an elongated pavilion and its 'atrium' just plain open space, since the 'L' is also independent from the surrounding buildings. The row house is an even easier case, because the rows do not form a perimeter block and are never repeated; even if it were, each house would still be separated from the other – by at least 12 inches.

dirty

HIGH

LOW

HURRIC.

rotates because of
earth's rotation

COLD -50° air
is sucked
dum to
hot ocean

STRATOSPHERE

HOT

EAN
'S UP

E

The
Hurricane
(A
Catastrophic
Thought)

A category 4 hurricane hits the Mexican peninsula of Yucatán and spurs the following catastrophic thought – bolstered by my new understanding of the *potential limit conditions*[1] of human occupation of the moist prairie:

> Extreme suburban fragmentation has led to systemic isolation (the holey plane). Lack of coordination by both city and county of vital protection systems is the further result of internalised logic and external laissez-faire that dominate each of the component city systems (the jurisdictional border between city and county). Suburban deforestation in order to construct streets and parking tarmacs everywhere has created an endlessly uncontrollable surface – a giant wind and waterworks – the setting for the perfect storm. Simultaneously, the proliferation of monocultures and destruction of biodiversity has produced an archipelago of opaque and self-satisfied fiefdoms (each use pursuing its own relentless errand). Shoddy construction due to lackadaisical supervision has resulted in a vast landscape of substandard firetraps vulnerable to any storm of the slightest severity (substantiated by the extensive property damage following each tempest). The euphoria of progress thanks to the obvious proliferation of 'the good life' for most income groups is a recipe for catastrophe: a refusal to see potential systemic dangers – the result of the unprecedented agglomeration of alphabetic root-components from subdivisions to landscaped gardens (the never-ending expansion of cutesy houses and their artificial accoutrements).

1. In the early stages of writing this book I narrowly missed the collapse of the overhead electrical grid which caused enormous problems during a more recent hurricane described in the final chapter.

Weeks of extreme ozone alert: everyone aside from
an underpaid security force is confined indoors. Children
and the elderly fill the hospitals. This health crisis, already
taxing emergency relief centres, is followed by a 500-year
hurricane that results in weeks of severe flooding far
beyond the theoretical flood plains. With prolonged black
outs, extreme heat, humidity and destruction to shelter
caused by devastating winds, entire communities are in
utter disorder. The drinking water supply collapses,
instigating a health crisis much like a flu pandemic, in
turn aggravated by the engineered landscape, which
now functions as the disease delivery system. During the
incomplete mop up, emotions run high, conflagrations,
looting and violence are an everyday occurrence. Gated
communities serve as readymade prisons or bastions
of defence against marauding gangs of the increasingly
frustrated and lawless. Collateral tragedy: escaped
environmental toxins, polluted drinking water, epidemic
sickness, extreme stress. Total inundation.

Tropical Storm Allison 2011 (flooding)

Abecedarium

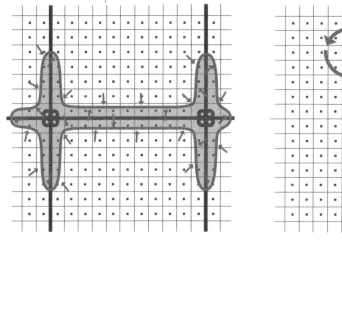
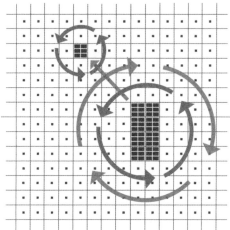
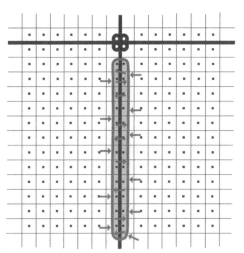
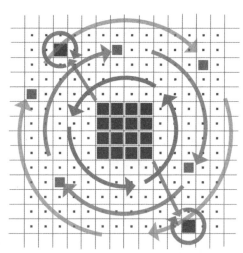

Development Dynamics on the Houston Field

With the addition of weather to the forensic toolbox, I will now turn the exploration to its vast other – the *field*. This is the ground across which weathers race and upon which the megashape sits like a billiard ball poised to roll, along with the many other object-like-phenomena. Hägerstrand, the Swedish geographer, viewed his practice centred on the bindings between these phenomena, the most relevant of which he refers to as 'base elements'. Similarly we recognise among the field-objects a number of base elements, some fixed, some mobile, all 'packed' more or less loosely together. The field, in this sense, is a galaxy of bodies in various states of flux.

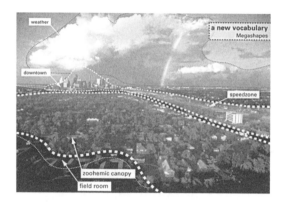

Megashapes

To conceptually rein them in, a crude diagram of forces attempts to depict the flux, followed by an abecedarium reflecting on the elements and their bindings. The abecedarium is a table of alphabet letters that for centuries has allowed students to commit the fundamental structure of language to memory. Likewise, reading the city requires a metropolitan alphabet, a collection of base elements fundamental to the character of the middle landscape. In more recent vocabulary, these are known as *topological spaces* or *topoi*. Three- and now occasionally four-dimensional, these elements, like the artfully drawn letters of an ancient abecedarium, form clusters of human invention worthy of investigation. Compiled here are specific metropolitan letters found in Houston, but prevalent elsewhere as well, from single-family houses to subdivisions to 18-wheelers to freeways. Yet it is absurd to think that an entire alphabet could ever be constructed, thus mine remains idiosyncratic at best. Entries are divided into four categories – moist prairie, subdivision, speed zone and streamers – followed by miasma as a coda.

As a coda to these alphabetics, I have come to realise that all the components never remain discrete. The result is an alphabet soup in which the broth is more potent than its ingredients. The metabolism of the modern city forces all of its acts and actors, live or inanimate, to perform more or less willingly, much of it impossible to even begin to understand. Looking just at the dynamics of development easily reveals an enormous complexity: the original grid, still housing downtown and parts of midtown, is rapidly thwarted by the freeway supranet; add to this the mixture of activity, each rather independently seeking the most profitable location; and the location itself a complex play of American distance and lack of regulation; 11 hospitals fighting for space and dominance in the Texas Medical Center – together yet apart. Four gas stations holding down each corner in a street crossing in the speed zone – together yet apart. Agglomeration economies at work. In the meantime commuters, consumers and producers crowd the roadways forcing observers like myself into a schizoid shifting of the gaze – from the moving and the momentarily fixed, but always before or after the fact, either speculating or filling in the colours.

The most limiting aspect of the array of words is that on the field they all form complex sentences, particularly when observed in time. These stirrings in the soup centre around all forms of mobility: the freeways spawn frontal road speed zones of various sizes and economic forces; the sub-centres as attractors produce a concentric developmental turbulence; avenues, bulging at the seams between traffic and subdivision become corridors of intense commercial activity. In fact every intervention – large or small – produces ripples and occasional tsunamis on the Houston field. In the abecedarium most of this must be read between the lines.

American Distance

Moist Prairie

The moist prairie occupies large portions of the Gulf Coast region from Louisiana to Texas. (In Texas this zone consists of some 20,000 square miles including estuaries and bays.) The prairie is pockmarked by open pools that serve as evaporation basins for the very clay-like 'gumbo soil' (named for the regionally popular seafood soup). Covered with dense grass, Loblolly pines (more recently, planted oak) and beautiful flowers, drained by deltas of bayous and populated by birds, snakes, alligators and myriad insects, Houston's moist prairie – despite modern abuse – remains in rare parts a wondrous world.

Bayou

Snaking its way across the moist prairie, the bayou is the ventilation system of the prairie's various waters, from settling humidity to tropical downpour. Slowly, the bayou carves its serpent-like body into the gumbo soil. When its curvatures join, oxbows are formed, leaving banana-shaped pools of stagnant water filled with rich, primordial pond life. Before the Army Corps of Engineers petrified the bayou, its ecology was an astonishing array of flora and fauna; thick greenery along the banks quenched its thirst. The source of the bayou is the watershed hidden below the ground of the delta. Managing this complex of prairie, bayou and watershed, peppered with suburbanisation, is as complex as the management of life itself.

Delta of Bayous

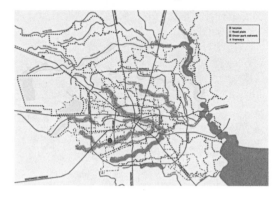

After a deluge, drainage of the nearly flat prairie takes three forms: a very slow seeping through the gumbo soil, solar evaporation and runoff via the delta of bayous leading to the Bay of Mexico. In Houston the delta once dominated the moist prairie, but this natural condition is long gone. Exchanged for aggressive manmade modifications, expertly implemented by the Corps, the new bayou is not in fact a bayou, but a crude runoff ditch of paved concrete chutes – a natural and cultural disaster.

Fieldroom

Houston's living room is the seemingly endless space formed between the underside of the tree canopy (see: Zoohemic Canopy) and almost flat ground. Generally taken for granted by drivers, this vast interior is a fortunate side effect of the planted forest in the areas between the delta of bayous. Dappled light, tree trunks, the slightly undulating floor and occasional bridges crossing bayous provide drivers with a spatial treat beyond the reach of even the most ambitious architect.

Flooding

Tropical storm Allison hit Southwest Texas on 5 June 2001, dumping 37 inches (1m) of rain during a five-day torrent that blanketed the entire Houston area. The most expensive storm in the city's history, it is estimated to have cost the region almost $5 billion, and 22 lives were lost. Rumour has it that Ebola and other deadly viruses were floating in the streets around Texas Medical Center, which for the second time (and unwisely) located its animal testing labs in the basement, which promptly flooded. The punishing storm sat directly over the centre of Houston for days. Two-thirds of the county was inundated. Despite extensive flood protection developed over many years, technology and government failed miserably.

Amidst current concern for global warming, it may be redundant to note the abuse of nature that characterises all modern settlements. And in light of the intelligence possessed by organisations such as the Army Corps of Engineers, the reasons for the disaster might seem obscure. However, the long-standing habit of engineers to define problems in the narrowest of terms (avoiding or flatly denying potential side-effects in order to make an unencumbered final decision) and thus omit externalities in final cost-calculations, is probably the origin of many environmental disasters. Much like carrying out military missions, each problem is compartmentalised; for example, flooding can be solved by 'getting floodwater from one point to another in the fastest and most cost-effective way'. The refusal to understand flooding as an environmental problem with global consequences is devastating. Citizens and government are infantilised by a knowledge structure that cultivates professional expertise. Yet flooding is a cultural issue, the management of which hinges on our interaction with the environment we have chosen to inhabit. Manipulating nature is local meddling with global consequences. Today Houston is moving ahead, in leaps and bounds, thanks to new science, sobering experience and a renewed interest in the life of the fieldroom.

Harbour

Once the runoff waters have gathered, the arteries of the moist prairie empty into the wide waterway leading to the Gulf. Here in the harbour, the city, the state and a major part of the nation meet the world.

Jesse H Jones became the first chairman of the Houston Harbour Board in 1914. His leadership and the confluence of the Spindletop oil discovery, the formation of Texaco and the opening of the city to the world through its new harbour consolidated Houston's global importance. His role as director of the Reconstruction Finance Corporation (RFC) and his creation of Fannie Mae in the late 1940s (he must be turning in his grave today), combined with the car industry, air-conditioning and highway building, spurred enormous urban growth during the postwar period. Despite the importance of the airline industry, the Houston Ship Channel and its umbilical connection to the energy industry remains the city's main lifeline. Here sea and land are brought together around millions of containers – stacked high on ships and distributed on 18-wheelers. The second-largest harbour in the nation, such a littoral cavity is an open wound to mother nature. If catastrophe strikes, the entire region grinds to a halt – maybe for months – yet recovery strategies such as we have seen in New Orleans are sorely inadequate. Harbours are not simply technical installations but mediators between land and sea.

Landscapes

Three types of landscapes unfold below my window on the eighteenth floor. To the right, a newly refurbished public park (one of the few inside the inner loop) boasts a public golf course – a willed, exemplary version of the moist prairie. Next to the park and directly below my perch, a swathe of green and a simple brick structure with on-site parking (shaded by a corrugated tin roof) borders pasture divided by rows of trees and decrepit fences – a minimally cultivated moist prairie. To the left, a third landscape of tightly packed houses forms what JB Jackson would have called 'a modern version of the vernacular landscape'. (A fourth landscape is barely visible beyond the public park: a ragged swatch of prairie grass and a couple of scrawny pines. It's not much to talk about – an odd blip on the plane of the field – but nevertheless essentially characteristic of the holey plane.)

Constructed according to the latest methods in creating pseudo-natural ecology, the park features smooth hills and interconnected, barely articulated evaporation pools as well as gulleys (mini bayous) for run-off. This piece of artificial nature reveals how a group of dedicated citizens can transform the ragged lacunae in an otherwise built up area into something resembling the indigenous moist prairie. Adjacent to it, the vernacular landscape, with its agricultural striations,

describes the mixture of city and hinterland that characterised early settlements. Considering the bulldozers idling next door, its days are numbered.

Today, the upturned field is left untouched because of rain. Stripped of its last bounty by a flock of white egrets, it is the last stand of agriculture. Birds will congregate until the surface water has evaporated (which takes four days longer than in the park) but soon work will resume: raw gumbo will disappear and the pouring of a thin concrete slab will signal the arrival of suburbanisation. A jump-cut ahead in time and a new housing project has moved us into the twenty-first century.

The leisure landscape of the park and the suburban ground zero of concrete illustrate two diverging trajectories: one towards complete striation and artifice and the other towards smoothness and the natural. What would happen if these two extremes worked together in unison? Would the vertical organisation of the built become slurred by the curvilinear motion of the smooth?

Oil Refinery

To the east on my horizon is Texas City, a 'city' of refineries. On 23 March 2005, BP's Houston refinery sent a plume of smoke thousands of feet into the air – something between a mushroom cloud and a smoke signal. The conversion process had gone haywire, leaving 15 people dead and 100 more injured. Breaking up the crude oil chain – using boilers in which the column of various products separates to allow cracking, unification and alteration to produce further derivatives – is a complex and delicate process. An accident occurred when the octane level of a batch of oil was pushed a level too high. A micro-cosmic parallel (both poetic and sinister), the refinery explosion foreshadows the 'superheating' of the entire region – just waiting to blow. And when it did – now at the ocean floor miles away in the Gulf of Mexico – BP's sinister history of failure in Texas City and beyond reached its most spectacular conclusion.

Storm

Each city has its own disaster scenario, a version of 'the perfect storm', some worse than others. Yet all are characterised by the collusion of natural and artificial events. Los Angeles and the San Francisco Bay Area have their earthquakes, brush fires and mud slides. Phoenix has heat and drought, the South Coast (from Texas to Florida), hurricanes. The Midwest experiences tornadoes.

Mexico City undergoes thermal inversions while the Randstad in Holland must barricade against flooding from deforested rivers far upstream in Austria and Germany. Because of size and complexity, human settlements now shape their environments – tainted by certain levels of manufactured toxicity – the result of a clash between nature and culture.

When a storm rides in over Houston from the southwest, inundating the moist prairie, it is a vast natural system's (unsuccessful) attempt to compensate for our technological intrusions. The result is a recurring 'natural' event that has characterised this part of the South Coast for longer than we can remember.

Suburban Prairie

The complex relationship between agriculture and suburban development in Houston is telling. There was cotton until the market collapsed; then the entrepreneurial spirit saw an opportunity in the moist prairie. With the added irrigational capacity of the bayous, rice growing came to the fore – this was before India could feed itself. It was also the second, more radical start of man's intrusion into the ancient ecology. Soon the swelling surface of the moist prairie, with its archipelago of ponds, became inundated with rice paddies. On their way south, migrating birds began to rest and harvest here. But eventually agriculture was displaced (though some defiantly remains) by suburban development and outpaced by 'better' venues for rice crops in the emerging global marketplace. Today, the paddies are (mostly) gone, while the birds still come – perhaps hoping stubbornly that the rice will return. The new 'agriculture' of the suburban city is the grass-plantation; and crabgrass the ground cover of choice in a city of the third kind.

Zoohemic Canopy

A planted forest of oak trees shelters large portions of Houston's moist prairie. Never in history has an effort to plant trees by private individuals and groups of citizens had a greater impact on the public and private environment. The collective impact has so far been uneven – it was motivated by self-interest. Consequently, much in the way that elevation indicates economic status in New Orleans, the canopy's density reflects the economic status of its beneficiaries. But like most human interventions into the natural world, the canopy produces unforeseen consequences. A steady airflow that ventilated the moist prairie for eons, streaming from the southwest onto open grassland almost made it habitable. The loss of air-circulation resulting from the zoohemic canopy was compensated for by the introduction of air-conditioning. This reveals the complex risk in manipulating the prairie: the canopy which appears perfectly natural is in fact almost as artificial as the technology that replaces a cool breeze.

Subdivision

Roughly around 1900, coinciding with the first great twentieth-century technical revolution, human civilisation forced the prairie out of its natural state. Both were unprepared. For a hundred years, nature succumbed while civilisation took command. The second major encounter occurred 50 years later. If the first era was dominated by electrification, motorisation (there were more vehicles with piston-driven internal combustion engines in Houston than in any American city) and the mass-marketing of such new inventions as the bicycle and the safety razor, the second era was characterised by the refinement of earlier inventions including commercial aircraft, air-conditioning (of utmost importance for Houston) and frantic suburbanisation. It was also the era of insured mortgages, leading builders to switch from developing only two or three houses to entire subdivisions. This led to radical intervention into the workings of the moist prairie and the true beginning of its agony: the developer city. Distances were extended but simultaneously shortened by increased speed, in the airways and on the new freeways. Paradoxically, the only place of relative calm was in the subdivision itself.

Today, traffic still slows upon entering the subdivision. Development is still regimented through uniform platting – a single-family house is separated from the next identical house by an identical distance. The rigid internal grammar of the house is still intact, if writ larger. Everyone moves according to unbending schedules. From 6.30 to 8.15 the SUVs roll out of driveways to embark on school deliveries and work schedules. At 11.00 only the whine and stutter of the leaf-blower is audible. The subdivision (and its mechanisms) is the true cipher of suburbanisation.

Cul-de-sac

The overcoming of distance finds its ultimate expression in the subdivision in which all internal roads end in cul-de-sacs. Considering the American obses-sion with mobility, these spatial forms suggest an unfortunate neurosis whose therapy may reside in constructing a new frontier that expunges all cul-de-sacs.

Deed Restrictions

These limitations on property use are the legal apparatus that most closely resembles any form of zoning in Houston. Set by developers, deed restrictions and their restrictive covenants radiate outward from the subdivision and into the fringes of the surrounding speed zone. Once in place, they are often unchangeable.

Gated Communities

One possible reinterpretation of Ellfrit's suburbia (see Quiet Neighbourhood) is to think of his assignation of 'neighbour-hood' as something other than commu-nity. Living in the same neighbourhood is a reflection of economic status, not of a community constructed without propinquity. Renaming the neighbour-hood 'subdivision' pointedly refers to its geometry and method of plaiting – social reality is bracketed out. Conse-quently, the 'gated community' is not a traditional community but a reflection of common interests such as security and economic homogeneity. Often veiled in lifestyle concepts such as golf, age or marine activity, the human making of distance and necessity to create difference between inside and out (the home turf) is as ancient as the temenos of the first temple in the desert. This urge may be even more potent in the endless *terrain vague* of the suburban city.[1] Moreover its gates may in fact be the gates of the

143

traditional city, revealing that suburbia has never been very far from it, perhaps only redefining what qualifies as building material. Here, lawn becomes cobble-stone, trees columns and the leaf-blower a broom. Nature is kept at a 'safe' distance.

Lawn

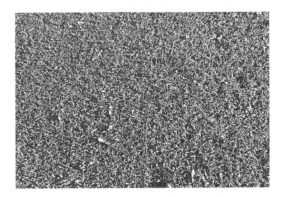

Breaking through the earth's crust, the first blade of green promises to fulfil the outlines of lawn. Each day, newly occupied territory turns green. Filling in and filling out, the undergrowth turns into overgrowth and instead of only tending, watering and fertilising, one must cut back. Trespassing the permitted limits of the lawn's rectangular confines is the threat of green's imperialism. The havoc of lawnmower stirs the suburban stillness.

Leaf-Blower

The hysterical rattle of a two-stroke engine and the reek of fuel disguise the emblem-atic significance of the leaf-blower – best seen in action blowing leaves and other vegetal matter onto the neighbour's prop-erty. The utter futility of erasing any sign of

1. The notion of a *terrain vague* (vague territory) was popularised by the Catalan historian Ignasi Solà-Morales in the late 1980s, referring to the sprawl typical of all expanding cities in Europe.

decay, the obsession with 'clean', the reckless expenditure of energy and an absurd reliance on technology to accomplish the simplest of tasks: ultimately the suburban arsenal of behavioural attitudes comprises 'passing of the buck'. Together with its operator, the leaf-blower forms the most synthetic 'weapon' of suburban existence.

Pool

Pool attendants constantly seeking balance monitor the chemistry of backyard pools – the precise measure of water, chlorine, pH, sodium bicarbonate and muriatic and cyanuric acids. These water doctors, of course, are preceded by pool-builders. Along with gardeners, lawn doctors, garbage collectors, tree pruners, maids and babysitters, these sub-disciplines form a veritable suburban maintenance force whose primary task is to uphold undisturbed stillness – the fixed eternal smile of domestic bliss. A transparent glass block held still in the hot and airless afternoon, the perfect pool lies in wait for the diver to break its surface and the liquid thrashing to begin.

Quiet Neighbourhood

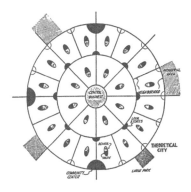

All cities harbour a particular diagram in their organisation – an often crude but effective way of depicting their 'diagrammatic' aspects. Houston has one such archetypical diagram which is astonishingly clear and remarkably able to absorb radical change while still retaining its descriptive power. The Federal Housing Administration's National Housing Act of 1934 – which for a brief but crucial moment in Houston's development history financed a series of instrumental subdivisions – expressed a middle-class vision.[2] For the sake of historical convenience, we can trace the first subdivision to Radburn in Fair Lawn, New Jersey of 1928, 'the town of the motor age'. It was quickly synthesised as the typical subdivision, the crucial planning unit of suburbia. The power of this invention is the synthetic assembly of ownership, open space, road, house and financial agility (it could be financed, built and sold under the auspices of available instruments and markets.) By the late 1950s, private development took the lead, still backed by federal mortgage programmes, which by now included the GI Bill and two highway financing schemes: the Federal-Aid Housing Act of 1938 and the Federal Highway Act of 1956. The same developers who began using architects shift to subcontracting everything from design to plumbing to building, leaving the architects in the dust.

The new cyclopean subdivisions required local public involvement, particularly in creating infrastructure such as schools, sewer systems, flood control and roads. All major suburban cities have had their boosters, movers and shakers. What makes Houston such an interesting case is that one of its more important

'seers' of suburban vision, the planner Ralph Ellifrit, understood what would appeal to the future suburban family – not only Houstonians, but virtually all future American suburbanites.

Ellifrit, the director of Houston's Department of Planning from the late 1940s to the early 1960s published 'Quiet Neighbourhoods' in 1949, in which he captured the essence of a privatised suburban world.[3] It was brilliant in its simplicity and forecast of Houston's future. Possibly derived from developments such as New Jersey's Radburn, designed by Clarence Stein and Henry Wright, or from the work of English planner Ebenezer Howard, the father of the Anglo-Saxon suburbia, Ellifrit's concentric diagram condensed his sources to a bare minimum. His vision was composed of 'neighbourhoods' (ie, subdivisions) linked to a combination school/park and surrounded by a loose master-grid – the super block – that would feed directly into the freeway net. Although local stores were less significant in the diagram than a set of prominent 'community centres', it is a matter only of exchanging their uses. With a more prominent location and size, these 'stores' would eventually yield the modern shopping centre.

Ellifrit made the scale-change from house to subdivision largely in response to traffic flow and congestion. By the late 1940s, the number of traffic accidents was 'staggering and something had to be done'.[4] Ellifrit discovered shrewdly (as did his favourite developers) that when it

---

2. As part of the New Deal, the FHA launched a programme to 'encourage credit for home financing' and so revive the badly depressed building industry. Thus, the FHA insured mortgages up to 90 per cent for low-cost houses and 80 per cent for houses costing at first up to $16,000 and later up to $10,000. Adapted from Kenneth Jackson, *Crabgrass Frontier: The Suburbanization of the United States* (Oxford University Press: Oxford, 1985).

3. Ralph Ellifrit, 'Does Houston Need More Public Housing?', *Houston Chronicle* (29 Jan 1952), Section I, 6.

4. Ibid.

comes to suburban urbanism, the coalition between public and private interests is fundamental. Exploiting the problem of traffic congestion with the assistance of federal highway dollars, the profitable union between infrastructure and subdivision emerged.

What Ellifrit understandably failed to anticipate was the ensuing population growth, subsequent proliferation of suburban services (referred to as 'central business' in his diagram), and emergence of a polycentric city. But this 'failure' is also his diagram's strength, because its most striking features are generosity and openness. As a blueprint for action, its message was clear: all a subdivision required was an embedded school doubling as a park, a connection to the intra-subdivision grid with its supporting facilities of 'shops' and 'community centres', and subsequent connections via an extended concentric system of roads leading to the central business district. These labels have since been reinterpreted and greatly modified. Much like the grid of Manhattan, the innate 'generosity' of Ellifrit's diagram has given room to a new city, while remaining largely intact.

Row House

Cheek by jowl, row houses stand barely a foot apart. These so-called town homes have invaded a block of the inner loop. It is not particularly strange since land prices have been rising, building stock is getting old and a younger market is afoot. The old single-family bungalows of the traditional wards are the first building type to be displaced. Two per lot, each town home is two times the size of the original bungalow, but with half the number of occupants – although the population has remained the same, building bulk has quadrupled. Negating the typology of the original row house with direct access to the street via sidewalks, clusters of row houses are fenced in and entered from the back through electronically operated gates. Outer suburbia invades the loop, bringing fear and security concerns to formerly open neighbourhoods.

From the windows of my high-rise apartment I can sketch a rough map of the relative land costs by focussing on building types. Single-family houses replaced by row houses are one indicator of rising land costs. Or so it seems – in the emerging speed zone at the unruly edge of the freeway, real-estate speculation is rampant. Virgin land is planted with high-rise buildings, lonely single-family houses remain, strip malls are erected, long abandoned gas stations lie forlorn, town homes are built in the shadow of the towers. This is the soft underbelly of the real-estate market: the prevalence of building types other than the single-family house indicates that we are no longer in the subdivision. But there are other ways to escape its confines...

Single-Family House

Sitting roughly at the centre of the lawn, the American Dream – plagued by gender politics, night and day domains, child and adult territories – is the emblem of suburban life. Its magic is astonishing since sameness is what allows each family to locate its own specificity. As the single greatest investment in a family's life, its plan and organisation dominate. The single-family house is tattooed on our imagination (like the car), suppressing all other forms of dwelling (or transportation systems). As a form of habitation, it casts a long and dark shadow on a concept of community beyond family and friends.

SUV

The sport utility vehicle (SUV) and its accessories (television, cup holders, satellite radio, GPS) is not only the ultimate suburban vehicle, but a symmetrical reflection of the single-family house and its increasingly sophisticated household technologies. Philosophically and psychologically, its size and apparent security make the SUV a direct extension of the house itself – or at least its nomadic other, a roving compensation for the cul-de-sac. House, vehicle, driver, inhabitants are bound together in a network with many branches: shopping, education, work, faith, leisure. All predictable elements of a roughly generic metropolis. But all this may now be in the past and only a prop in the increasingly virtual American Dream. Silently an electric car lulls the subdivision even further into silence.

Time Out

The flatness of Houston's middle landscape is deafening – only bumps and grinds, the abecedarium of objects and activities, cut the silence. The original prairie must also have been dominated by silence, only occasionally broken by rainstorms. Utter flatness negates all depth or thickness, obscuring the dimensions which make the prairie a complex environment. Naturally, this flatness is best understood in plan, from above. But such convenient distancing lowers the experiential magnitude of the holes in the holey plane. Maps and diagrams represent these gaps well, but it is moving across them which establishes their holey-ness. To appreciate fully the discontinuities of the metropolitan experience we must stop briefly and turn to the in-between, to 'the gap where the garment gapes'.[5] Not concerning Barthes' original reference to eroticism or voyeurism, but rather the perversion of skipping over precious 'text' of the city – almost imperceptible in the traditional city where every space is occupied. On the prairie land is abundant, hence disposable. But there are other forms of discontinuity (often related to these gaps), disruptions or 'bumps and grinds' that dot the endless field. This is the alphabetic city. Contrary to Mark Kingwell's suggestion that cities are 'collisions: of natural conditions, material forces and human desires' (for argument's sake, taken literally here), in the middle landscape there is an innate tendency to avoid collision.[6] Here each 'letter', whether a subdivision or poly-centre, abruptly ends – not with a sharp edge (the walls of the medieval city), but through sheer difference in entirely unrelated and often incompatible function – especially prevalent without zoning. The study of this type of 'fracture in the text' is best done using a traditional architectural device: the section.

In the subdivision, at the outer edge of the cross-section, speed sleeps quietly under the hoods of cars and SUVs stopped on parking tarmacs. This state has been reached only after zooming along the freeway, then weaving through the speed zone along a feeder still at considerable speed, until slowing into the subdivision. The freeway's frenzy never stops, while the subdivision's interior is frozen in time. The discontinuity suggests that its calm is forced – only truly captured in the numerous photographs of the house: the family in front of the car, friends gathered around the barbecue. There are albums entirely dedicated to immobility, which in reality is momentary stasis in a field of flux.

At the other end of this spectrum lies the freeway – the physical artery between home and work, home and shopping, indeed home and world. Here the cinematic takes command. Using speed as a measure, the centre-line of this section is the unglamorous wall separating the two-directional freeway, cutting both ways as it were, across the middle ground of feeders and franchise strips to form the speed zone which stops abruptly at the edges of surrounding subdivisions. This speed zone – the essential organ of physical communication in the middle landscape – is placed between subdivisions, which form the most essential domestic core.

Bound together in varying proximities and modified by technological prosthetics, from skateboards to 18-wheelers, humans and their hardware are immersed in this everyday circularity of speed and stillness. The spectrum of mobility even extends to rates of acquisition, with new car models appearing at freeway speed compared to real-estate turnover along adjacent feeder roads, which slows to a standstill in the neighbourhoods beyond. It is as if dominant restlessness – the endless drone of traffic – has unsettled all stability, all attempts to create predictability and order. Of course, this implies that despite geographical discontinuity, the middle landscape is still the arena for urban collision.

5. Roland Barthes, *The Pleasure of the Text* (1973), trans R Miller (New York: Hill & Wang, 1975), 9–11.
6. Mark Kingwell, *Concrete Reveries: Consciousness and the City* (New York: Viking, 2008), 13.

Speed Zone

In the late 1940s the Texas Highway Commission undertook an immense construction programme, much of it in Houston. By 1980 the city had over 200 miles of freeway – spoke and wheel. The network of suburban freeways contemplated at a remove from its setting is a singular feat of engineering – a grand tribute to the expansionist spirit of suburbanisation. Constant geometry elevates technological prowess to the highest form of reason in the tattered landscape. Freeways rule the metropolis, just as sewage rules the traditional city.

When immersed in Houston, it does not take long for the obsessive character of its freeways to come into mesmerising focus. Negotiated at top speed, the human parade of suburban culture is here most vigorous and most determined, yet paradoxically, most dependent on technology. The denizens of the freeway have become its product, users transformed into victims. Commuters on a subway train passively submit to the indignities of underground life, while drivers on the freeway enact the very form of the network. No longer kibitzers, they are performers in the theatre of mobility.

In Texas, most freeways are bordered by two parallel frontage roads which feed the endless commerce distributed in repeating clusters of franchise outlets, forming a linear city – soon a thousand miles long. The result is a network of speed zones that dominate the metropolis at its major trunk lines. Houston's freeways form a spoke and wheel system, now augmented with high occupancy lanes and a series of semi-private toll roads. The formerly smooth prairie is today pulled, pushed, tweaked and twisted by the reckless force of mobility, whose destiny no one can predict.

151

Gas Station

When you find one, you know you are in the speed zone. Long before Starbucks completed sophisticated market research on demography and education to identify the best locations for their coffee shops, oil companies studied the flow of traffic to find theirs. Fundamental to the franchise equation of the speed zone, gas stations mark peak areas of activity. Once you find one gas station, you will find others – often kitty-corner across the intersection. Since the oil business is the most global of industries, you will feel at home wherever you are, because as long as there are vehicles, there will be gas stations.

Sign

Speed and pulsating images open ever so briefly onto one fantasy island after another, creating the potential for a highway-euphoria in which gravity and space disappear. Built shapes recede fuzzily into the distant horizon. Nearby buildings and other drivers appear as mere images, fluttering bodiless in the corner of the driver's eye. All navigation is reduced to a lexicon of propelled matter and highway hieroglyphics, in which we – once pedestrians – are projectiles with sensibilities both haptic (at our extremities and backsides) and visual (in our heads). Weightless, we hurl through the highway ether, encircled by a galaxy of promise.

Speed Zone Kirby

In the central portion of Houston's inner loop, Kirby Avenue is a prominent thoroughfare perpendicular to a major freeway (Highway 59) and extending north–south through the city. It is typical of tributaries in the feeder system around the freeway network. Like a python that has consumed a mouse, the internal pressure of the speed zone causes adjacent subdivisions to bulge and, in the case of Kirby, even push into the suburban fabric. The linearity of the typical speed zone is often augmented by reurbanisation projects that form distinguishable megashapes. Since there is no zoning, the buffers that emerge seem natural developments – the push and pull of commercial activity – and when too invasive, the speed zone is held back. Precisely how this occurs is buried in real-estate history, yet this transition zone appears natural compared to planned areas, which give the impression of being pressed up hard against each other. The speed zone eventually encounters hidden constraints: relative freedom slowly adjusts itself to the deed restrictions of the adjacent subdivision. Here the view changes from cinematic to photographic, from movement to stasis. Firmness (subdivision boundaries) and flow (along the speed zone) comfortably co-exist.

Perhaps Houston's internal connections become apparent only after a catastrophic event when we discover that behind its superficial cacophony lie vital mechanisms upon which the entire metropolis depends. In the everyday, however, there is virtually no evidence to support this. At close range our megashape reveals only tiny events – thousands of simultaneous but independent actions, the ebb and flow of humans, vehicles and artefacts; from soap to hamburgers. All seem entirely disconnected, each action on its own errand, each event oblivious to every other. Much as in a Samuel Beckett novel, actors (and their paraphernalia) seem thrown haplessly together by chance.

Yet because of common physical limitations or jurisdictional grounds manifested in the particulars of the street, plot system, social habits and mores, these metropolitans are all functionally similar. A complex network connected by friendships, work habits and chance builds a rich mixture of activity. If we look closer, complexity increases: next to the laundromat, a small Thai restaurant cultivates astonishingly different behaviours, attitudes, smells, sounds, gestures. All together, hundreds of tiny uses and associated events combine in the landscape of the observing mind to create a symphony of sights and sounds which no plan could duplicate. It is clear, also, that these micro-activities are purposeful; supported by financial institutions, service mechanisms, individual know-how and desire.

A dense stim of stims happens simultaneously and with frictionless ease, aside from small hesitations in entryways and at intersections. ET Hall describes the same natural proxemics in an image of a flock of birds resting equidistantly on a telephone wire. The density of the stims is of particular importance here. Only in highly concentrated megashapes is stim density roughly equal. Behaviours and actions in many of these settings are unified into different families of activity: business, shopping, health, dental care, etc., producing distinct monocultures. By contrast, along Kirby, a variety of events and behaviours, thoughts and speech, is the norm.

Like a toppled Tower of Babel, in the Kirby corridor a thousand tongues speak (not only in different languages but also with different intentions). Observed outwardly, these conversational scenes may seem quaint, but here they nurture democracy and equal opportunity. In the nooks and crannies of the visually discombobulated microcosm, careers are made, enterprises started, bodies trimmed, stomachs satisfied, risks taken, affairs consummated, business transactions conducted, tax returns prepared, apartments cleaned, high-fives exchanged, coffees imbibed, children taught to read, hair cut, nails manicured, cars washed, shoes mended, art sold, books signed, clothes fitted, TVs tuned, loud music played, beer drunk, barbecue slow-cooked, cars valet-parked, wallets misplaced, petty crimes attempted, parking tickets written, umbrellas opened, winks shared, kisses thrown, cellphone messages delivered, barbells hoisted. The speed zone comprises a distinct socioeconomic ecology.

The density and complexity of activity within the Kirby speed zone represents a communal good – something to which any city worth its name aspires. Here we encounter the complex machinery of emancipation at work. This is the power filigree – the 'open work' of human interaction, short on capital but essential for the life of the small entrepreneur, which makes democratic cities worth their salt. And perhaps best captured by French philosopher Michel de Certeau in *The Practice of Everyday Life*, which outlines the tactics that motivate our daily lives.[7] Governed by the 'handgun' of minor real-estate deals (in comparison to the 'big gun' real-estate strategies of surrounding enclaves), this fine-grained, chaotic, constantly changing swathe is crucial. Thousands of independent, overlapping personal stories make up this tattered web, so complex as to be uncontrollable and impossible to reproduce. This is the reason Certeau clearly distinguishes between everyday tactics and governmental strategies.

Planners and high-volume developers (with the exception of gasoline companies) carefully avoid these corridors of exuberance. In fact, the microphysics of activity in this naturally evolved enterprise zone is more similar to life in the old European city than the suburban city.

Speed Zone Greenway

Immediately to the north of Kirby another swelling occurs in the speed zone around Highway 59. The year is 1980, the spokes and wheels complete, the developer Kenneth Schnitzer and his Century Development Corporation begin to buy, house by house, an entire middle-class neighbourhood at top prices. Once it was all bought up and subdivision deed restrictions had been changed to allow commercial and housing, one of the largest mixed-use centres – Greenway Plaza – appears. The various official descriptions drawn from websites reveal these expansions as 'enterprise zones' with a distinctly marketed self-image, a fictionalisation essential to the establishment of 'competitive advantage'. The plaza itself is a case study in suburban reurbanisation:

> Greenway Plaza, Houston's premier masterplanned business development, offers an environment which is uniquely tailored to the needs of today's business community. The unique style of Greenway Plaza's campus combines a central 'inside the loop' location, efficient floor plans, professional management and an unparalleled group of amenities.

Working professionals and visitors to the campus have easy access to The Shops at Greenway, which include a unique selection of retail options and a full-service food court.

> The Renaissance Houston Hotel with 388 guest rooms and the Greenway residential condominiums are also located within the Greenway Plaza campus. Manicured landscaping, reflection pools and sparkling fountains add to the beauty of this distinctive business address. Greenway Plaza features over 60 acres of prime frontage on the Southwest Freeway (US 59), providing an easy commute to the Galleria area, River Oaks, West University, Texas Medical Center and downtown Houston. No other address in Houston offers so many services in such an ideal location.[8]

What the description does not reveal is that Kenneth Schnitzer, the developer, was Gerald Hines's greatest competitor. Greenway Plaza motivated the latter to leap further out to take an even greater risk and a huge portion of the city with him – with great success, as we will see.

7. Michel de Certeau, *The Practice of Everyday Life*, trans. Steven Randall (Berkeley, CA: University of California Press, 1984).
 8. http://www.greenwayplaza.com/home/aboutus.asp

Galleria

Along the Inner Loop we encounter a further swelling of the speed zone, often signalled by traffic congestion and known as the Galleria. Houston's largest in-town shopping complex is the result of a new era in the city's real-estate history. The Galleria is where Gerald Hines, who cut his teeth along Richmond Avenue, began thinking big. Probably before anyone else, he saw the enormous potential of the prairie stretching endlessly to the horizon. Thus he conceived of a new commercial centre for the competing city and outlying county, located right at its dividing line. The Galleria literally emptied downtown of its street commerce, recentring the entire region and even international shopping, on a level almost approaching Hong Kong in its heyday. Today shoppers are exposed to as many foreign languages as can be overheard in the Texas Medical Center or in downtown, the world's energy capital.

Lacking a coherent infrastructure, the overall result of clashing grid and cul-de-sac is (for architects) disappointing, messy and plagued with inadequate access, traffic congestion and lack of public amenities (only one measly skating rink in this Mecca of Shopping!) A recent urban design gesture, a set of stainless steel arches (crochet loops reminiscent of Saddam's Baghdad)

attempts to direct the shopping stream, but is effectively only a type of mascara – inadequate to solve major organisational flaws. The problem? A brilliant real-estate concept generated minimal response from architects and the city planning department. To exacerbate the situation, various spurts of expansion similarly lacked foresight and understanding. A spectacular opportunity to create the ultimate shopping city, a surplus heaven augmented by office space, hotels and housing, has so far been wasted. There are several valiant schemes for commercial subdivisions underway that may result in local success, but overall the truly sloppy Galleria megashape simply lacks the clarity of downtown. But as always in Houston, the story is not over yet. In the long run, smaller shopping outlets will have an easier time competing; any development that localises traffic lowers the pressure on the road system by reducing unnecessary mobility.

Yet this critique is the architect's perspective and bias: the fact is that the pragmatics of the motorised city allow no time for the in-between, or rather plenty of time for these jump cuts because the destination is more important than physical contiguity – after all with a GPS any destination is easy to find. Here

156

finding a destination is just like switching channels on TV.

The power of the speed zone, stemming from the coupling of freeway and surrounding feeder roads demonstrated by Kirby, Greenway Plaza and the Galleria, shows the fundamental role increased mobility along this supranet has, not only in the dispersion of housing, but on the systematic atomisation of all urban functions. In the end completely restructuring the centralised city – probably forever.

Streamers

Location, location, location goes the real-estate mantra. Yet the distribution of almost equally spaced access-points across the entire plane, lubricated by speed, characterises the modern metropolis. This smoothness is warped by an erratic real-estate market, leapfrogging, deed restrictions and the lack of planning. Buildings and their uses drift, often recklessly, as if in invisible hands. These become streamers, defying common practices, refusing the seductive animation of speed zones, corridors and strips, and often hubristically taking risks, stranded as often as breaking new ground. Here availability of land and prize may be the pressure points while location plays second fiddle.

Airport

Suddenly Houston is the centre of the world. The airport marks the symbolic presence of the world cities in suburbia, unreachable in the past but now always within reach, just as the highway promised to overcome the original split

157

between city and suburb, the globe is now in our backyard. Across the tarmac of its landing and take-off runways, longing is embedded and intimately connected to distance – to lines of flight. As a strange manifestation of the promise of the city, airports have themselves become facsimiles of cities (non-places according to Marc Augé), devoid of any sentimentality like place and community yet with their own permanent denizens from airplane spotters to customs agents. With its paranoid protection systems the

modern airport is the most elaborate manifestation of the gated city. Although Houston has two major airports, there are also eleven others, many of them private. The accident rate in these smaller, more affluent airstrips is considerably higher than in commercial aviation. From postage-stamp spring-boards, airborne nomads inspired by crop-dusters launch themselves beyond Houston's cul-de-sacs, defining the outer limits of suburbia's reach.

Downtown

Lit up twice a day by the rising and setting sun, downtown glows like a giant candelabrum. Jutting boldly out of the suburban field set vertically against it, its towers, despite individual design, size and location nevertheless form a jagged whole. The grid upon which the towers stand is square and neutral, a perfectly 'democratic' playing field. Yet in plan, section and profile, the towers radiate corporate power, successful speculation, aspiration, progress – a message thoroughly undemocratic. The elevators in Houston's downtown descend below street level, to connect with an air-conditioned network of underground tunnels leading to garages with direct access to the freeway system and subdivisions

beyond. Banished to the street are the service people: delivering goods, waiting to clean an office tower or to take the public bus. Class is literally inscribed in the towers, the street and the tunnels below: vertical integration with lateral separation.

But these striated conditions are changing radically in almost every downtown along the southern edge of the United States, particularly in Las Vegas and Los Angeles. The Houston Downtown Coalition, a non-profit organisation with planning and implementation capability, is slowly but surely modifying impediments to openness by reinventing the street as common ground. Eventually the energy industry office park will become a real down-town, and as has happened before, the geography of openness will change.[9] The Coalition understands that the neglected street is the true battleground of a great city; where the public, by tradition and instinct, gather, linger and commune.

Although downtown may still occupy the graphic centre of Houston, it will never become the centre of the metropolis – the atomisation of the city's activity is already complete. Cut loose from the city-suburb equation, down-town thus becomes a streamer.

Corridor

After the speed zone, the corridor may be the most ubiquitous form of 'location' in the endless middle landscape. Its genealogical relation to the strip is obvious. In Houston the Metro, the city's public transportation agency, has taken the lead by naming a whole series of 'office corridors' using the lightrail tram as a spine: North, East End, Southeast, University and Uptown. The proliferation of corridors may indicate that the polycentric city, too, will be left behind – in the middle landscape everything must move: people, traffic, business, real-estate, location. The most established of these corridors in Houston is the so-called Energy Corridor, which has gathered together all major energy-related companies of the world in a loose formation rambling around the major highway crossings in the western end of the city – a speed zone overlay. A short mission statement by one interest group indicates how corridor associations are formed:

Founded to help guide the success of member businesses, the Energy Corridor District is made up of area members, staff and an elected board of directors who work with public and private organisations at the local, regional, state and national levels to facilitate attracting, relocating and optimising the success of Corridor companies.[10]

---

9. Earlier change was driven by Central Houston, Inc under the able leadership of Robert Eury and his former partner Guy Hagstette, in close cooperation with the city and the many companies that settled in downtown.

10. http://www.energycorridor.org/home/

Eighteen-Wheeler

Jackknifed, a long-distance rig creates disaster on Hwy 288: live chickens mingle with stranded motorists, diesel oil spills onto the road surface. Long-haul truck drivers are modern road-warriors with too little sleep, delivering to the nation artichokes, lettuce and tomatoes from California; Mercedes-Benz motor cars from Alabama; beef from Chicago; trinkets made in China and imported via Long Beach harbour; mangos, avocados and watermelons from Mexico; polo ponies from Lazy-F Ranch; and more 18-wheelers, piggybacked and hauled by 18-wheelers from El Paso to dealers in Ontario, Canada.

Escapists

The long escape trajectory that began for Europeans as a dangerous ocean crossing and eventually 'ended' in suburbia became an object lesson in 2005 when millions of Houstonians took to the road to escape approaching hurricane Rita. An interesting conceptual shift took place. As escapes go, this was the last leg. Prior escape from city to suburb was suddenly forced to a conclusion – Leonard Cohen's question as to where the highway leads had found a blunt answer. The utopian dream of paradise in suburbia was odiously shattered, for as long as Houstonians will remember. For some the motorised 'escape' took 24 hours of driving, at one mile per hour, often with no terminus but a rather anticlimactic return to the city unscathed. Rita landed further east. We are rarely shown, with such clarity and minimal consequence, our need to forge a new relationship with the moist prairie.

Faith-Based Community

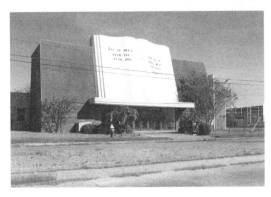

It is pure speculation to claim that millions of inhabitants miss the traditional city's public domain, especially since Houston never had it. Yet there are many compensatory systems that provide communion for those seeking it. The basic desire for civic community cannot be killed off entirely, even here. With tongue in cheek, I call these compens- atory urban forms 'replacement therapies'. Some are so effective that they may forever obscure an actual need for the public domain: such may be the case of religion and its many outlets. The Lakewood Center in Houston is proof positive. Its website proclaims:

> Jesus brought the gospel into the marketplace, the village square – everywhere people gathered, and the Lakewood International Center will become the 'village square' of Houston. With more than 2 million people currently attending events each year, there is hardly a more visible or familiar landmark in the city. Its location alone will allow us to present a message of hope to more people than any outreach in the history of Houston.

> Today, it is a sports and concert arena. At the Compaq Center, millions of people have watched the most gifted sports figures and entertainers in America. Its history has been one of excellence, crowning champions in the world of sports.

> And continuing in that great and awesome tradition, The Lakewood International Center will become a place that will crown 'Champions of Life'.[11]

Lakewood Church inaugurated its 16,000-seat auditorium on 16 July 2005.

11. The Lakewood Church, previously located outside Houston's inner loop, has moved inside it and so joined the general flight back to the city. The former Compaq Center, a sports and entertainment venue, has been transformed into the Lakewood International Center. http://www.lakewood.cc/pages/home.aspx

Several million people visit each year, which makes Lakewood the largest church in the country. Through direct reference to the ancient village square of the Holy Land, Lakewood equates the traditional community life of the public, shared by all citizens, with the 'village square' inside its own church, although here only the messenger (Pastor Joel Osteen) and his flock have entry. Gone are the Romans, the moneylenders, the hawkers, the kibitzers – in short, the citizens. All have been replaced by the *flock* (or *tribe*, in nomadic terms), which includes psychiatric counsellors, child-care workers, disaster relief agents and their spiritual leader.

This subtle sleight of hand transforms 'the public' into the 'semi-private' space populated with 'Champions of Life'. Likewise, in the suburban metropolis city policemen have been replaced by 'security', and public land privatised. A faith-based spiritual domain has been seamlessly joined with the socio-psychological domain. The ubiquitous non-governmental organisation (NGO) takes over for the city, erasing both it and society. Beyond Lakewood's spiritual square – and an assortment of other pseudo-squares of varying interests – lies only the *system*: the streets, parking lots, runoff technologies and endless freeways. What is left is the city of a third kind.

High-Rise

The icon of American urbanisation, the high-rise or skyscraper, has a special role in Houston. Despite its poetic soubriquet, in real-estate deals the skyscraper is a crude barometer of land price, the ultimate capitalist tool. It too succumbs to aspirations and fads. Its priapic nature appeals to CEOs who see fortunes not only on their balance sheets but also in their brand. In Houston the high-rise has always been at the forefront of speculation and thus appears in the oddest of places. The high-rise in which I live is a reminder of the reurbanisation of suburbia. Conceived as a condominium, it has remained a predominantly rental building, awaiting a more profitable turn in the market. At 35 floors with an extremely efficient floor plan and floor-to-ceiling windows it is a beauty.

Homeless

At the lower end of the housing spectrum (many steps below suburban middle-class types) is *virtual housing*, sites where the poor have staked out a place to huddle in a park or under a bridge. Bizarre as it may sound, in Houston these ephemeral loci reflect a suburban humanity too.

The homeless are barely visible here. In the case of the solitary man occupying a bench, rain or shine, night or day, on 'my' street, the homeless are oddities, blips at the edge of the suburbanite's windshield, driving by. When my 'neighbour' leaves his bench (to shop? to eat? to relieve himself?), he leaves behind a grocery cart and 'stuff': a folded umbrella and blanket, the most rudimentary marks of habitation. His back always turned to the street, he lives without the accoutrements of the American Dream. He looks relaxed, well fed. Out on a stroll he is free as a bird; the new Diogenes, the last pedestrian, Benjamin's *flâneur*; in his isolation and utter solitude, the ultimate suburbanite. This insight sharpens in the context of another suburban metropolis.

Until recently, 40 per cent of America's homeless lived just south of downtown Los Angeles. They flocked around social service outlets, stores and improvised piazzas. Many lived there by choice, the extreme version of DCI (Development of Common Interest) – a tent city lining the sidewalks, each tent separated by tiny but equal side yards. The settlement hauntingly resembled a subdivision, the Tudors and Georgians replaced by various types of tents, from upscale North Face models to homemade varieties.

Ironically, the 'lot' was the sidewalk, a public margin almost extinct in suburbia, porch-phobia having given way to TV-room-security, suburban paranoia. Although the tent city inhabitants behave differently to their suburban counterparts, the setting is identical to the gated community, here surrounded by a police presence providing the traditional *cordon sanitaire*. A human tragedy approaches uncomfortably close to conceptual farce. But the new downtown Los Angeles cannot afford any blemish, so the subdivision-lite has been shut down, its denizens sent packing. The poverty of form in the suburban design imaginary is startling. Rich and poor alike occupy the same solitaires, held in place by the same militant divisions.

Industry

Industries that in Ralph Ellifrit's theoretical city were neatly placed at major intersections of ring and spoke, have, like all alphabetic components, found their own logic. The oil industry has settled along the ship channel, other industries related to transport and storage along major rail and freeway interchanges. But the false conception of total access has led industry to follow land prices as often as location, leaving large swathes of industrial zones spread evenly through the middle landscape.

Motel

The last reiteration of the tourist camp (invented sometime in the first three decades of the twentieth century) manifested in the tourist home, the cabin camp, the cottage court, the motor court, the inn and the highway hotel, the motel is no longer common along the interstate highways and is now found in the speed zones of the motorised city. Hovering, in terms of class, between the Greyhound bus rider and the air traveller (who frequents Hiltons and Holiday Inns), the motel guest is car-bound, notoriously male and itinerant. Multi-storeyed but still with ample parking, the Motel 6s and Hampton Courts serve the last four-wheeled road warriors and nomads. The hum of the highway is their ocean, Tom Bodett their Beckett.

Museum District

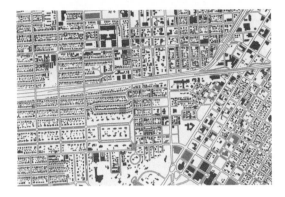

The Museum District loosely assembled in the area surrounding Montrose Avenue is a misnomer. Historically, 'district' has always implied a territory under the jurisdiction of an administrative power of some kind – a magistrate or council – but not so in Houston. Here under the free will of the suburban market, 'district' and 'centre' (as in, Texas Medical Center) have taken on entirely different meanings. Merely geographical, a 'district' transformed in suburban lingo is a swarm of institutions frozen in unpredictable spatial configurations. By contrast the Texas Medical Center (TMC) is a throng of hospitals fighting each other for territory, yet jealously sticking together.

Buried in the annals of real-estate history, the creation of these loose formations remains obscure. But it appears that the bonds drawing elements together in 'district' and 'centre' are motivated by an 'economics of love and fear' (to paraphrase Kenneth E Boulding). 'Love', because it is nice to be able to visit each other (the public may feel the same) and 'fear' of not being identified as a member of a distinguished fraternity because located outside of its influence. Such halo effects are the end result of suburban development practices, since there is no central power to assign contiguous space for a collection of museums, and location is left to the relative softness of suburban fabric and the shrewdness of land developers ('if there is a will, there is always a price').

Much like the TMC, the Museum District began with one major land purchase around the Museum of Fine Arts in the late 1970s. Land for the institution's expansion was bought by the Brown Foundation, marking the important role of cultural philanthropy in the increasing sophistication of a city with rapidly growing wealth. The foundation recognised that creating *lebensraum* for institutions is essential to making them prosper. This may have stemmed from attempts, possibly by some foundation members, to create what Stephen Fox calls 'islands of order' in the wealthier subdivision which eventually led to the introduction of deed restrictions. The foundation also bought land for the Museum of Contemporary Art, and by the late 1980s the area surrounding the museums became a recognised district, now augmented by the very successful Natural History Museum and the Children's Museum designed by Robert Venturi.

At the outer edge of the Museum District halo, another cultural philanthropy under the leadership of art collectors John and Dominique de Menil had already begun to assemble land. Working closely with the architect Louis Kahn, the Menils quietly laid claim to a super-block formed by Richmond, West Alabama, Mandell and Montrose. At the time no one could predict that they were initiating a new museum of international significance that would put Houston, the energy capital, on the cultural map. The museum designed by Italian architect Renzo Piano opened to great acclaim some 20 years later in 1987. (It should be noted that the doyens of the Museum District *and* Houston's master builder began their empires simultaneously along Richmond Avenue. The Menils are progenitors of an internationally re-nowned institution; Hines is a global developer operating on several continents.) The Menil Museum, like Gerald Hines' Villa Savoyes in the Richmond Corridor, is a true Houston building – with a roof aping the zoohemic canopy by design, drawing an exquisite dappled light across the magnificent collection. Piano repeated and evolved the canopied roof in 1993 in a special gallery for the artist Cy Twombly, in an effort to insert minor eddies of cultural activity throughout the housing-dominated Menil super-block. That was just the beginning – major revision of the block is under way today.

Parking

The inverse of the motorised city (its dark, silent, petrified side) is the parked city. Here hulking metal, lacking freeway bravado, lies still. In suburban four-car garages, in driveways, along streets, on huge expanses of asphalt or concrete tarmacs ('strands of hell' during summer), in urbanised precincts and in underground garages. In the city, the human body and the automotive body are relentlessly repeated, the former at its desk and the latter in its parking spot. Unless heavily scheduled 18-wheelers, most of these vehicles sit more than they move – slowly leaking effluent onto temporary resting places. This inactivity prefigures the final demise when all of the glass, metal, plastic and rubber ends up in the wrecking yard or refuse dump, adding to a growing body of dross. The parking complex, especially when empty or only partly occupied, reminds us of the final moment of our demise, when all mobility ceases – when centrifugal force lays its turbulent appeal to rest and all is quiet. Parking is the iron lung of the metropolis. Without its assistance everything else would come to a halt.

Private Club

Suburbanites in Houston undertake many compensatory measures to overcome distance, including the formation of 'artificial communities' such as private clubs. Often supported by very expensive membership fees (and held in place by walls, gates and guards) they provide likeminded occupants of similar socio-economic strands the opportunity to meet, often under the guise of leisure. With the addition of tennis, swimming and exercise programmes, the gated subdivision invents its other – the private 'public square'.

Richmond Corridor

In the early 1950s a young developer named Gerald Hines recognised Richmond Avenue as a potential commercial boulevard, running east to west.[12] This was also the beginning of the enormous growth of cities all across the country – all pointing west. Perhaps inadvertently, Hines had conceived an office-dominated avenue as an upscale evolution of the traditional strip, replete with abundant landscaping around each building and a central esplanade.

12. For an extensive analysis of the corridor's evolution, see: William Middleton, 'Modernism Meets Richmond Avenue' in *Hines: A Legacy of Quality in the Built Environment* (Bainbridge Island, WA: Fenwick, 2007), 47–64.

With the skill that has now made him a legendary developer, Hines perceived the value of high-quality design in commercial development. For architects this was a heady era, especially for the firm Neuhaus & Taylor. In their capable hands, modernism had a brief but exquisite encounter with the suburban city. The buildings Neuhaus & Taylor developed may have been the only time in the city's brief history that a real Houston building type evolved. It may have had conceptual origins in Le Corbusier's Villa Savoye, in which the car is parked on the ground floor of the building sitting on *pilotis* above, serving as both car park and house. Finding a true habitat in Houston, a flock of these westward moving villa-émigrés serves as an artificial extension of the zoohemic canopy. The Richmond Corridor has remained roughly untouched since the mid 1960s. Hines, in competition with the young developer Kenneth Schnitzer, who built an entire mini-city along Richmond (See: Mini-City), leaped even further west to construct his own city-within-the-city – the Galleria. The Office Corridor, as a new linear intensification, was but an elegant intermezzo in the steeplechase for bigger and better. However the Corridor – as a new linear intensification away from the supranet of freeways – is born here, although along Richmond its glory is short-lived.

Strip

The venerable American Strip survives in the backwaters of the motorised city, where it is overtaken by the speed zone. Sheltering the not yet franchised, the odd, the weak and the marginalised, the strip is the dustbin of the commercial zodiac. Here amidst video outlets, porn shops and low budget bars, revellers find strip joints (Gentlemen's Clubs). Strangely, these establishments have a stronger global than local reputation – attracting mostly out-of-town visitors.

Strip Mall

Numerous erratically distributed swellings of development, not exactly megashapes but larger than the typical pavilion, speckle the surface of Houston. A veritable menu of urbanisation has emerged, ranging from symbolic manifestations (a lone high-rise in a sea of subdivisions) to the mini-city and everything in between. The strip mall is the most ubiquitous of these forms, sometimes trumping a gas station or pharmacy for a corner location, otherwise content to take three or four lots on a frontage road. Minor franchises compete for space within the unique establishment, often survivors from the past or younger upstarts (Lola's Nails & Perms). Strip malls betray the familiar characteristics of the almost defunct shopping centre – but are leaner, less capital-intensive, closer to home and more conducive to a quick in-and-out. The old hitching post has come back to haunt us.

Storage

'There is five times more closet space than there was 50 years ago', writes Alex O'Briant, former Rice graduate student. He continues: 'A general trend indicates that further acquisition in the domestic environment is generating a centrifugal effect upon storage. This movement has bolstered one of the largest growth industries: self-storage facilities. There are 38,833 self-storage facilities nationwide, including 694 in Houston alone. Facilities average 38,183 ft² and 268 units, making up a total rentable area of 1,291,845,439 ft² or 4.59 ft² per person.'

Space Centre

The late Robert Crosson, a Los Angeles poet, told me how his family 'went west to California' from Oklahoma at least four times – always returning empty-handed. The Crossons viscerally experienced the end of nomadic momentum. It is difficult to know whether such experiences at the literal end of western migration had any role in the invention of the space programme. Nevertheless, onward momen-tum has since been brilliantly resumed on the Gulf Coast in southeast Houston. In September 1961 NASA chose this as the location of its primary research and development centre for testing spacecraft and other systems related to space exploration. Later named the Johnson Space Center (JSC), it remains emblematic of the nomadic nation's next frontier.

Texas Medical Center

The Texas Medical Center, one of the more distinctive megashapes of the city, is a suburban oddity – a subdivision inflated and compacted with the aid of some super-steroid to produce a true monstrosity. Suffering from total neglect

170

of the overall environment, TMC must have been designed by allergy doctors. Consisting of 15 hospital systems agreeable only as far as occupying roughly the same location, it is an example of urban lobotomy in which each system is cut off from all others, even the common road network. The seams between each hospital are rough at best, forcing staff, service personnel, the sick, the infirm, their guardians and the occasional visitor to follow inadequate signage as they navigate streets, flyways, endless corridors and underground passages. Truly an ailing city, the Medical Center cries out for a major restructuring. There is an eerie parallel between modern medicine's persistent refusal to acknowledge holistic theories of health and obliviousness to the fact that a well-designed environment enhances wellbeing, assisting all participants in the process of healing. Doctors and medical engineers designed the operating theatres and forgot all the rest.

White Collar Prison

For developers faced with rising land prices, the four-storey apartment complex enveloping a multi-storey parking garage becomes the building type of choice. Ironically, these apartment blocks derive their form from the perimeter block of the traditional city. Fenced in with a single entry and exit via the garage, their capacity to construct a city is dramatically arrested – the building is only a large pavilion isolated from its context. Peculiarly similar to the penitentiary, with guards at all points of entry, the apartment blocks house a rapidly expanding white-collar workforce. Denying all forms of democratic collectivity in favour of socioeconomic tribalism, sequestered suburban thinking permeates all aspects of the attenuated metropolis.

The Woodlands

In Houston the impact of oil on suburban development has been much more than supplying a market of house buyers. In fact, the first major middle-class subdivisions such as Friendswood south of downtown (and later Kingwood to the north and vast tracts to the west) is developed by Exxon in the early 1960s, to be immediately followed by George P Mitchell's The Woodlands – 25,000 acres of rich and poor living in harmony. Today all this is but quaint history, Mitchell's own debt problems and market collapse have rapidly drawn his utopia into the stark reality of David Harvey's 'flexible accumulation' maybe for a very simple reason: not even one of the wealthier oil men can build a city since financing such an enterprise is enormously complex. Here state, federal government and banks (using every new-fangled financing tool under the rubric of 'securitisation' to replace 'flexible' with 'merry-go-round') combined with major corporations have to join in a magical dance while the market snaps at their heels and regulators sleep in their dens. In the end the result seems inevitable, as foretold by such able observers as Joe Feagin writing in his *Free Enterprise City* of 1988: 'Thus, Mitchell's surplus capital will likely create another upper-middle-class residential suburb of Houston, but one with its own facilities.' The only correction we may have to do to his prediction is to erase 'middle' in light of a new and substantial cohort of super-rich Mexicans moving into The Woodlands in an escape from the drug wars further south.

Miasma[13]

It has stopped raining. Stepping from our air-conditioned office building out into the dense, humid air of Houston summer, I am hit by an acrid *smell*. Or rather, my nose notifies me of the acrid smell, which directs my memory across the canopy of trees to Texas City and its refineries beyond the horizon. Industrial surplus has invaded our city, carried on a barely noticeable eastern wind. My companion and I comment on this, and the thought lingers even as the smell fades into the everyday.

Spatiality begins in the short distance from nose to brain. My body, a minor geography of sensitivities, from sight to smell, disperses me. The smell that signals distance from the refineries is also radically dispersed, dramatically permeating the entire city: I assume it smells everywhere. Suddenly, the spatial limitations of my eyes are overcome by my sense of smell. Toxicity fills the entire geography of the settlement much like a giant elastic organ, without a visible casing. Smooth and cloudlike, this smellable domain describes the spatial condition of the metropolis better than any visual measure could – particularly because the smell is carried by a myriad of discrete particles, forming an immense roving cloud. Likewise, the eternal *sound* of air-conditioning rules all interiors in Houston, from car to bedroom. Humming spaces form an archipelago of cool islands, each with its own envelope and capped by a roof. Some two million pitched roofs and more than three million car roofs, stamped out in factories, are linked to Texas City by that sound of blowing air. Add to this constant buzz the *noise* of the road, at times sonorous like a river and at other times accentuated by racing siren decibels, sharp screeches and blunt thumps of abruptly arrested matter – drawn from any number of calamities. With road noise comes smoke, both typical car exhaust and that from collisions. Factor in the pain of flesh pounded by collapsing metal and we circle back to the body's geography.

13. *Miasma* forms the coda to the abecedarium to suggest that it is not capable of containing many aspects of the metropolis, particularly if they don't have a precise geographical locus. The word 'miasma' is chosen with reference to the ancient Greek belief that ailments derived from smells and gases, a theory which lasted into the nineteenth century and culminated in London's cholera outbreaks. History repeats itself in the metropolis, since we now believe that modern miasma is carcinogenic. The Greeks may have been right after all.

Sullying nature is an ancient practice, but when the metropolis is shrouded in a yellow haze causing eyes and throats to burn – sending asthmatics to hospital – modern pollution steps out of the haze of history to take on a vague essence, a permanent aspect of the metropolitan here and now. Raising temperatures and tempers in cities like Los Angeles and Houston, pollution causes climatic and experiential change: Houston smells faintly of mould, Los Angeles sunsets are saturated in technicolor. Merging with the seasons, a new climatic concoction is formed, whose impact on the environment is gradual and surreptitious. Residents come to know their conurbation by its newfangled smells and sounds, and the allergies it triggers.[14] Yearly dust clouds of yellow pollen enter into the city's respiratory cycles.

In this wide circle from the body's geography to the reeking refineries and back to the body's (psychic) site, an ephemeral space is discerned that is not commonly associated with the space of the city. Yet acrid smells, noise and other toxic ingredients form a *new ecology* – an immense and infinitely variable artefact that includes dust from industrialised agriculture (nitrous oxide, diesel fumes, manure, urine) as well as ozone, air and water pollutants. Regardless of class, income, age and ethnicity, everyone shares this undeniably democratic condition. First appearing as an excess, it has become a permanent atmospheric fact of daily life that casts a pall across the fixed smile of the settlement.

Will citizens call, in unison, for a sustainable environment (the overused and enigmatic euphemism for metabolic

14. But there is more: the body is not just geography, but a psychic site. It, too, is affected by the ecology of toxicity. Pollution joins the dark side of *suburbanity* measured in statistics drawn from a variety of sources: fear (gated communities and elaborate alarm systems), isolation (of teenagers and the elderly in subdivisions, not to mention restless empty-nesters), environmentally induced illnesses (asthma and sinus afflictions), obesity (lack of exercise in car culture) and the daily frustration of the endless commute (34 years per day collectively in Houston, somewhat more in Los Angeles, less in Phoenix) take their toll.

174

balance)? Who knows? So far, amidst political posturing, wild assumptions and ensuing promises, no one is willing to pay. Suburban conurbations, dominated by weak government and individualism, do little to spur collective action. Yet if we mark the *frequency* with which 'sustainability', 'global warming' and 'pollution' recur in everyday conversation and media, it may only be a question of time.

Concluding the abecedarium, miasma is not strictly alphabetic, but it is grammatical in the sense that it infiltrates everything it comes into contact with. Much like a hurricane, miasma assaults the middle landscape and forces its citizens to instigate involuntary narratives. To varying degrees we are all affected by the acrid smell that is proxy for all types of pollution. This realisation makes clear that the abecedarium is not capable of fully describing the characteristics of the field in all of its dimensions. Furthermore, miasma reveals that the physical alone can no longer describe these characteristics. Opening the door to the atmospheric suggests that our visual apparatus is inadequate, and must be augmented by all our senses. The smell of Houston detected upon arrival at the airport is much harder to fathom than the downtown megashape, but it is nevertheless distinct. Slowly but surely, this type of 'software' threatens hardware in a descriptive hierarchy, implying that the collateral damage of the modern conurbation may provide us with a better understanding of the middle landscape than any past obsession with the single-family house or so-called sprawl. In this sense, the miasma is a metaphor for the future towards which we now turn.

The Self-
Organising
City

After selectively foraging in the endless field, an obvious question arises: What about the future? Although hurricanes and tropical storms pose a threat, turbulence of another kind agitates everyday life in the vast suburb: plans, projects, ambitions and rumours impinge on the environment. Predictions of this type have much in common with fiction – they may be entertaining, if not always accurate.

A turbulent present *reality*, rather than a futuristic or fictional city, is more interesting than either. Reading recent stories by the futurologist JG Ballard, I sense fatigue. How many dystopias can one stomach? Even William Gibson, the neuromancer himself, has returned to the present. When I pose my dilemma to Ed Dimendberg, he writes: '…I am not sure you need to invoke dystopian futures. Isn't the cruddy present sufficient reason to try to do things differently?' Yet increasingly, I do not believe Houston is 'cruddy', just un-evolved, a giant pubescent body in a continuous state of becoming. There is a further complication: the unruly city, especially when burdened by human real-estate mechanisms, appears nonlinear, dynamic, relentless, apparently unstoppable and unpredictable. Turbulent. There is no one in charge. Just as I stood bewildered before Houston's geography, when I first arrived, now, years later, I find myself perplexed when I confront its *making*. As is my habit, when facing a dilemma, I follow the Symbolic Interactionist dictum to 'go look' and, more precisely, to 'go *back* and listen'. I visit two informants: Joe Powell, director of the University Research Institute and John Mixon, a prominent land-use lawyer teaching at the University of Houston. Both are students of dynamic systems.

Powell tells me about the life of the corporation (Houston harbours at least 100), and in particular the demise of planning for the reason outlined above: there being no way

181

to predict the future. He describes how Jack Welsh, the maverick General Electric CEO (who retired from the organisation leaving $80 billion in the till) dismissed a huge staff in the 'futures department' in favour of research and development. Similarly, Japanese corporations abandoned their 1000-year plans from the 1960s and a decade later gave up on 100-year plans to rely almost solely on R&D. There is $24,000 of R&D in a Toyota; in a comparable Chevy only $8,000.[1] A Toyota Prius, rolling to a silent stop at a red light in Berkeley, California, foretells the future better than any ten-year plan. Rejection of the future is refreshing, but in the depths of a recession it should make us uneasy too: do corporations avoid the future in order to make the most of an opaque present?

Over the course of my career I witnessed the steady demise of the masterplan, though not necessarily in city hall, where the message often arrives last. Progressive planners such as London's Richard Rogers and Barcelona's master builder Oriol Bohigas, who learned from Ildefons Cerda (the builder of Barcelona's nineteenth-century *ensanche*, in which a wide grid of streets prefigured the emergence of the automobile though Cerda knew only horse-drawn vehicles) have known of its unhealthiness for a while. Although comprehensive plans are still made, they are often dramatically redrawn, after, by filling in the colours describing what actually happened. Masterplans projecting a future are always hopelessly wrong. Plans with lesser scope are even more prevalent in the form of Planned Unit Developments (PUDs) – frozen snippets of the latest market intelligence already on the road to obsolescence (but fundamental in the making of postwar Houston).

1. This text was written long before the recent demise of General Motors.

182

In the Americas the genealogy of the post-facto plan dates back to the Leyes de Indias (Laws of the Indies) signed by Philip II of Spain in 1573 but issued in definitive form only in 1680 – when all colonial cities had already been built. A self-fulfilling prophecy with a secondary effect, the US Land Ordinance of 1785 laying out the Jeffersonian grid still helps us to comprehend the vast country today. Unforeseen consequences may exercise more lasting significance than the original plan itself.

Mixon brings all this into focus in discussion backed by a paper co-authored with Kathleen McGlynn, 'A New Zoning and Planning Metaphor: Chaos and Complexity Theory' (2007). They argue that the coupling of comprehensive plans and the Standard Zoning Enabling Act relies on the use of the wrong metaphor: 'The idea of simple cause and effect that works for linear systems breaks down when applied to nonlinear, complex, adaptive, dynamical systems such as weather and land use'.[2] The writers use 'spot zoning'[3] as an example of how judges make decisions assuming that 'long-term land plans provide a reliable standard for measuring validity of specific zoning regulations'[4] when such plans have been made defunct by continuous change. After extensive and thorough analysis of numerous zoning cases, they recommend replacing 'the traditional planning paradigm (based on reductionist logic) with a new management paradigm grounded in complexity analysis. Instead of planners' maps, we would rely on *multiple interpretations of an accessible bank of current land use information* that displays how land is actually used in a

2. John Mixon and Kathleen McGlynn, 'A New Zoning and Planning Metaphor: Chaos and Complexity Theory' *Houston Law Review* 42:5 (Spring 2006), 2.

3. Spot zoning occurs when a small area of land or section of an existing neighbourhood is singled out and placed in a different zone from

that of neighbouring property. (A park or school might be allowed in a strictly residential area if it serves a useful purpose to neighbourhood residents.)

4. Mixon and McGlynn, op cit.

5. Ibid.

particular geographical area'.[5] The conceptual proximity between their proposed 'management system' and Toyota's research and development department is uncanny.

The Self-Organising City

Turbulence. The neighbourhood is up in arms. Signs on virtually every front lawn scream: 'No Tower of Traffic'. The abrupt introduction of a strange attractor (a new high-rise) in a basically stable field provokes a response, because the type is radically different from its surroundings. If Houston had zoning, the proposed 25-storey watchtower (they can see into my backyard!) would be labelled 'incompatible use'. Here, it is just another example of the self-organising city, a mere eddy in the turbulence caused by the TMC. And despite their vigorously organised not-in-my-back-yard (NIMBY) action, the surrounding homeowners have no legal (only political or economic) muscle to stop the developer. Alternative actions: shame (how could you do such a thing?), threaten (you'll never work in this town again!) or buy out (instead, we will develop a park for the community). Nor can the city act – unless willing to bend to minority interests and risk complaints or preferential treatment – in this case, for wealthier inhabitants. 'Politics', as the developer Bob Schultz suggests, 'has replaced zoning'. But since this is a question regarding 'the constitutional rights of the developer to build on unregulated land' we find ourselves in a holding pattern, if not a perfect storm.

Looking west from my balcony in 2008 I see the southern edge of the Texas Medical Center. Cranes gracefully assist an expansion estimated to cost $8 billion over the next 10 years. To my left (to the south), a 35-storey residential tower is under

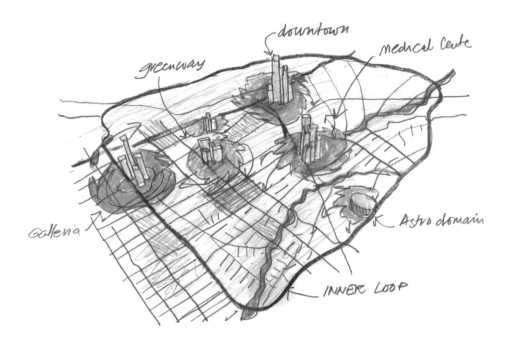

greenway

downtown

medical Center

Galleria

Astro domain

INNER LOOP

Turbulence

Subdivision

construction, as is, just below me, a second four-storey addition to the three-year old 'white-collar prison'. I speculate it will draw from the labour pool at TMC. What strange attraction does the City of Sickness and Health (that today conducts more operations than any medical centre in the world) hold for the relentless development of Houston? Turning 190 degrees at my perch, Houston's downtown produces similar stirrings in the fabric of its immediate surroundings, and much more obscurely on the subdivisions filling the gaps between attractors like the Galleria and Greenway Plaza. How do the power relations between attractors affect each other?

It is no longer a simple geography or assembly of megashapes emerging before me, but a *force field* dotted with centres of *turbulence*, fuelled by unknown quantities. I am taken back, as if in a movie rerun, to my graduate school days at Harvard and MIT. Names like Kenneth E Boulding, Jay Forrester, Muturana & Varela, Warren McCulloch, Gordon Pask, Marvin Minsky, Ilya Prigogine, Herbert A Simon and Heinz von Foerster roll by (like film credits) under the rubric of systems theory, cybernetics and self-organising systems. Youthful enthusiasm for the new has come back to pay a visit. But as John Mixon suggests, the problem is not, at least at this point, to describe the dynamics of the suburban metropolis in its own unique vocabulary, but rather to find a productive metaphor. Despite its very long history, metaphors still domi- nate theories of the city – from deceased bodies to dysfunc- tional machines. Larger than life – in fact far more complex than our own bodies, or any organic system – the actual city is a jerrybuilt patchwork of civilisation and nature.

If we postulate a relatively smooth landscape of development in which subdivisions are built at roughly similar intervals, suburban calm reigns. Then in one of the lacunae a hospital is built, then another and another, until 45 medically related facilities huddle around an invisible centre point. Over time, lesser elements scatter at an irregular periphery. We have landed in the eye of a development storm. Land prices are rising. The subdivisions and remaining cavities of undeveloped prairie are assembled to form greater parcels and new building types emerge: skyscrapers, white-collar prisons, row houses. Here the throng of hospitals has created turbulence. 'A mess of disorder on all scales', writes James Gleick. 'Small eddies within large ones. It is unstable. It is highly dissipative, meaning that turbulence drains energy and creates drag. It is motion turned random.'[6] The subdivisions, with their ordered universe of single-family houses, are threatened and pushed about by larger interests. But it is a random agitation. Remember, no one is in charge. Several of the weaker subdivisions are erased and replaced by higher densities.

The lacunae left from previous leapfrogging are filled in, particularly in the margins along freeways. Real-estate frenzy grows. Will they convert the rental tower into a condo? Will the old stables, clearly economically inefficient, withstand the pressure for new housing?[7] Without zoning, the turbulence has free rein – disorder and opportunity – real-estate heaven! Soon, the turbulence becomes status quo. The weak-hearted seek calmer pastures and no one is surprised. All this transpires in the world of the real and the realm of the visible.

Humans instigate this kind of turbulence, it is not the result of a hurricane. In this emergent view of suburban science, developers are *theorists*, the architects and engineers *experimenters,* and builders *equipment builders*. But all three groups need accomplices: financiers and land planners who, like truffle pigs, find and assemble the land.

6. James Gleick, *Chaos: Making a New Science* (New York: Penguin Books, 1988), 122.

7. In retrospect, they didn't.

Take the case of the Texas Medical Center. The instigator of real-estate frenzy (the truffle-man) was a businessman named Monroe Dunaway Anderson. In the early 1940s he thought that a medical centre should be placed next to the existing Hermann Hospital, which borders on a large park southwest of downtown Houston. The MD Anderson Foundation was established for this purpose and when Anderson died a couple of years after its foundation, a group of lawyers were charged with the distribution of the largest charitable fund created in Texas – $19 million. It helps to explain the suburban turbulence that resulted.[8]

The area around Hermann Park and the small hospital of the same name was solid and apparently stable when Anderson and later the lawyers began dreaming in the late 1940s. We can assume there is heated discussion in smoke-filled rooms. The temperature is rising. Rumour spreads and developers come around. Land planners, banks. There is a *phase transition* – the *still* suburban liquid becomes a *flowing* liquid. Numerous smaller eddies within the larger turbulence emerge, so that near a residential tower, gas stations, shopping areas and other commercial activity emerge. The inventors of the science around the 'strange attractor', David Ruelle and Floris Takens, invoked 'strange' for its psychoanalytical connotations.[9] Metaphorically suggestive, TMC is a truly 'strange' innovation in an otherwise slumbering part of the city that up to then specialised in housing for Rice University. In the environs of the TMC, far beyond the volatile liquids sloshing about in the laboratory of its creators, the strangeness is apparent. Who would have guessed the frenzy would lead to a new international health industry with ties to Latin America and the Middle East, astonishingly successful cancer

8. Gleick, op cit, 127–28.
9. Ibid, 132–33.

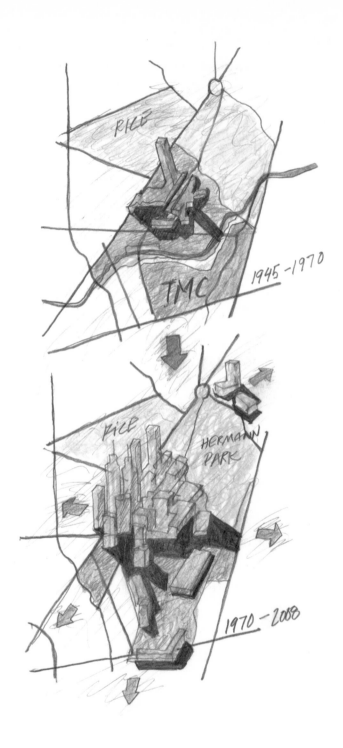

The Texas Medical Center Expansion, 1970–2008

research, a Museum of the Body and Natural History Museum, Children's hospitals and a Children's Museum (mixing TMC with the energies of the Museum District)? How can a city plan for this? The TMC and its ragged vicinity is an example of man-made self-organisation.

On the scale of the city we can assume that self-organisation overtakes planning in the traditional sense, although some management and steering of the development process takes place. Ellifrit's diagram of the late 1940s is much less a plan than a conceptual diagram and possibly a heuristic tool; it doubtless inspired few once its basic diagram had been presented. Self-organisation is frequently, yet erratically, fuelled by the reinvigoration or decay of attractors from new freeways to activity centres: TMC, Greenway Plaza, the Astro domain, The Woodlands, Sugar Land, the Johnson Space Center and the Galleria. Since the late 40s the ever-present turbulence has died down only a couple of times – once dwith the devastating collapse of the oil industry in the early 1980s – and then again in 2009, as before, a very dark time for theorists (developers), experimenters (architects) and equipment providers (builders) alike.

Returning to scan the activity surface, now taking into account self-organisation, activities – particularly among the movers and shakers – are clearer but not yet transparent. Amongst the ups and downs of daily activity, from commute to workday, we can imagine impending real-estate phase transitions like so many tiny tornadoes stirring across the prairie. Some will fade and disappear; others will form attractors. Meanwhile, the city is working. How can it run so smoothly? Despite the talk of ruthless competition there must be an underlying cooperation amongst the turbulence makers. Is there a hidden monopoly with which all major actors tacitly agree to cooperate? Or does an efficient road network, well-func-

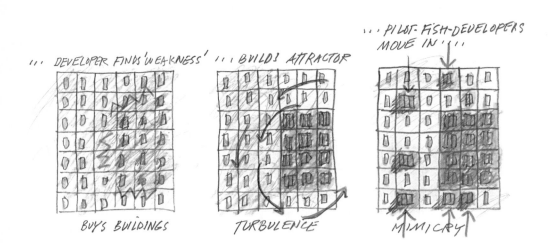

... DEVELOPER FINDS 'WEAKNESS'   ... BUILDS ATTRACTOR   ... PILOT-FISH-DEVELOPERS MOVE IN ...

BUYS BUILDINGS   TURBULENCE   MIMICRY

Block-busting

tioning legal system and abundant financing provide enough 'space and energy' for everyone to move through? Or something more mysterious, akin to the inscrutable behaviour of birds and bees? When this sort of swarming takes place, all actors behave roughly the same – comparing Houston to the world's biggest Monopoly game is to underestimate reality, whose arsenal of surprises far exceeds what the Chance card can yield in the game. However, there are features in Houston that provide its players with a level playing field. Its spatial generosity – the field's degree zero – is quite obvious: the flat, endless expanse and abundance of space. And although all hell breaks loose when an attractor succeeds, the stir remains local unless it is 'the big one'. But then again spatial availability kicks in and developers who can't take the heat leapfrog to scram for greener pastures – beyond the halo of the emerging attractor – which they find in due time. In the current state of the city's self-organisation, imbalance is the driving force of change.

Developer Culture

There is no shortage of imbalances in any modern city. Most are unpredictable, often volatile, yet essential to propel the modernity we have chosen to embrace. However there are stabilities too, which paradoxically may be the greatest source of volatility. Take the men and women who sprang the TMC on Houston, presumably a group of staid, sober lawyers who dreamt of changing the city and managed to reach the peak of development satisfaction. Over time, TMC has proved to be a new mini-city, with radical local effects as well as global reach. This lends credence to Houston developers' reputation as 'movers and shakers'. The result is equalled in magnitude and consequence only by downtown (the energy centre) or possibly the Galleria (shopping). All ambitious developers nurture similar desires: to construct the ultimate attractor that swallows all other contenders in its wake: or better, one that co-opts smaller, supportive eddies to make an even greater central impact. The gathering of energies which may or may not lead to a substantial attractor is an art marked by luck that Machiavelli recognised as *virtù* and *fortuna* (characteristics of the Prince). Modern developers rule the self-organising city.

On the subject of royalty in the postwar era, it is impossible not to begin and end with Gerald D Hines. As the developer of some of the most vanguard commercial skyscrapers, his may well be the invisible hand that still touches Houston's built imagination. Hines has both the first and final word on creative real-estate development, although it is a motley crew that motors self-organisation.

Houston's development in the postwar era could easily be a story of great men taking great risks to earn great amounts of money, but far more interesting is the story of how these developers have constructed *agency*, which, conflated with individuality and private initiative, has built a city of general success and utility. According to this secondary tale, the unregulated city may offer a formidable challenge to those who believe that good cities always require planning and regulation. But first, we must briefly consider the agents acting in the vast field of Houston, those operating in the immediate past just prior to the current recession.

Bob Schultz

The young and dynamic developer Bob Schultz, whose own background is in finance and English literature, agrees that modern developers may be truffle-pigs searching for the ultimate morsel (cheap land), but they must also contend with what Schultz calls 'pressure points', which requires that the pig be pretty smart (or at least have a special relation to *fortuna*). Schultz argues that pressure points impinge on the 'solution space', the sphere in which all energies must be gathered together to produce enough turbulence to instigate the emergence of an attractor. Failing this, the 'solution space' collapses and the project becomes part of real-estate history – or lore, if the collapse is loud enough. His five pressure points in any speculative venture:

1. Competition: other 'attractors' vying for the same morsels

2. Financing: developer reputation and the current economic climate – always conservative

3. Rules: regulations, codes and accepted if unspoken practices

4. Politics: because it has progressively replaced zoning, public opinion formed in neighbourhood organisations, among boosters and professional politicians, carries significant weight

5. Market: also closely connected to public opinion – the projected clients

Each of these points is autonomous. Competition has no understanding of financing and vice-versa, yet in combination they interact to create a contracting force field – like a tightening belt – attempting to squeeze the life out of

195

the solution space. If unchallenged, the force field consumes the energy, the developer licks his chops and moves on to the next attraction. If the force fails, the attractor emerges to wreak havoc on its setting (and to deposit a bit of change in the developer's till). All the while *risk*, as a form of meta-constraint, hovers around the force field. How much to risk? How much personal capital – both actual and virtual (ie, reputation) – to invest? Between perceived risk and Schultz's five pressure points, there is a certain levelling of the playing field. We must assume that all developers deal with a similar set of constraints that may lead to similar behaviours – all contributing to successful self-organisation.

I will later refer to these pressure points as autonomous agents acting upon the development process to form complex clusters of agents which shape the unregulated city. Risk aversion is a fundamental component of all development processes, but risk is also relative: some developers tolerate more than others. Shultz argues that developers undergo a maturation process in which the perception of risk-taking changes and is occasionally replaced by altruism. The ageing developer says to a younger colleague about a potential attractor: 'I either did the dumbest thing of my career, or I will succeed in what I always wanted to do for the city.' Because the city, its mayors, city council and bureaucrats – the custodians of its rules and politics – have all helped or hindered his success.

Frank Liu

Frank Liu's is a true Houston story. The son of an immigrant fast-food restaurant owner, Liu attended Rice University in Houston. When the economy collapsed in the early 1980s, Liu, in his own words, was 'too small, too young and too stupid', but lucky to have flexible financiers that spread his losses while 'much older and much smarter' developers went bankrupt. Today Liu is one of the city's more successful urban developers. Yet he will never forget the oil-bust induced 'sub-prime crisis' of 1982 that still has a dampening effect on property values in Houston and the consequent risk levels acceptable to its movers and shakers. In contradistinction to Los Angeles and Phoenix, Houston remains a 'conservative city'.

Once predominantly concerned with housing inside the loop, Liu's Lovett Homes now operates in the entire city, and has diversified to include commercial and industrial develop-ment. His mantra is 'build to suit'. Liu finds the land and an appropriate client, builds the desired building and leases it for the life of the business, often a franchise. The pharmacy or coffeehouse owners do their own marketing and Liu follows suit. All of these insertions in the rapidly developing field are minor attractors following in the halo of larger developments. This type of development relies on a relatively simple search engine that has a client in mind while looking for the right land at the right price, or the reverse. Then everything falls into place.

Liu's housing developments are a very different enterprise, in the arena of speculation and risk. (As a veritable Symbolic Interactionist he suggests that 'we drive around and look'.) He scours existing neighbourhoods. He finds those with both weaknesses (ready to sell) and potential (ready to build). He inserts a strange attractor that often shocks the neighbours. Along with increasing the quality, the price and the tax base, he also increases density by introducing a new building type – still within the American Dream parameters of a freestanding pavilion (two or three storeys on small lots), still with hard-wood floors. This is a much more complex enterprise than 'build to suit' since it is not only riskier but requires much more research, and much more foresight. Houston's peculiar development climate allows Liu to remain a pioneer – the first to think about neighbourhood renewal, the first to offer deals to land and house owners that can't be refused. His one regret – 'I never seem to buy enough land' – is seen in the ensuing development spreading in the wake of Liu's attractor. Smaller developers ride on Liu's prepatory work, like the tiny fish that swim in close proximity to the big fish, copying him if on a much smaller scale. Small fish survive on less.

Their opponents know Liu's attractors as 'gentrifiers'. Yet until we find a way to grow the economy without changing – the ultimate virtual economy – Liu's work is essential for the health of the inner city. And the competition from the outer edge of the metropolis is considerable. New housing precincts are not only new, but followed by new commercial services, new workplaces and new and better schools which together threaten to drain the inner city of its most valuable asset as a nucleus of work. In the meantime, the city imposes new restrictions on development: most recently the Parkland Ordinance,[10] in which a developer must set aside parkland or pay a penalty that is in fact an indirect tax on development.[11] Liu sees several problems: in his view there is no evidence that neighbourhood parks work since 'they are never maintained or occupied', and there is no coherent conception of open space, as it is closely tied to the endemic flooding problem.

Is this, I ask myself, a reflection of Houston's very nature as 'The City of One'? If we account for *private* open spaces filled

10. The ordinance, effective 1 Nov 2008, will require developers of residential projects to set aside land for parks or pay a fee into a park development fund – $700 for each single- or multi-family home. Parks advocates hailed the action as a vital step in ensuring that Houston's park system keeps pace with population growth. Leaders of development groups have argued that the requirements will drive new development out of the city. Mike Snyder, 'Houston council approves new parks ordinance', *Houston Chronicle*, 10 Oct 2007.

11. In the essay 'Obstacles' I will suggest that this 'fact' must be changed if the city is to rally around a common interest.

with lush greenery, stately trees and endless clumps of bushes, Houston is among the greenest cities in the nation. Neighbour- hood parks are politically expedient, but almost never placed where open space is needed for water retention, nor are they large enough to accommodate events and activities. (The abused and underdeveloped bayous come to mind.) An ob- session with parks in every neighbourhood was already reject- ed in Ellifrit's original diagram, where he located open space in connection with schools and nowhere else. Through taxes and bureaucracy, undue pressure is put on the housing sector to supply parks while industrial parks, office buildings and retail establishments are excused. In the game of taxes, regula- tions and controls, Houston's unique experiment in openness, in privacy, in self-organisation, in market economics – is threat- ened. Uniqueness is precious in a nation where conformity and similarity may be convenient for marketing – goods and politics – but clearly not as a way of life. Now, what happens to the concept of extreme privacy when a common threat appears? Will Houston have to radically change in order to face the carefully obscured question of the common good?

For Frank Liu, all new regulations which constrain the developer are a disservice to the inner city and will in the long run undermine its competitive advantage by hamstringing the open market. If the city instead concentrates on developing public transportation (he believes light rail is very desirable and important), better schools, better care for the zoohemic canopy (*Trees for Houston*) and the resurrection of the bayou domain and lets the self-organising school of developers do its job, Houston will prosper.

In other words, improve infrastructure, don't meddle in the private domain! The highway made Houston. Now *infrastructure* must evolve to support the ever-changing city. The social consequence of the current trend is towards striation, not openness and flexibility. The young, the empty nesters and the wealthy who can send their children to private schools flock to the inner loop while middle-class families live in the county – perpetuating the bifurcation of city and suburb and prohibiting true evolution.

Liu agrees with me that what is needed is a holistic metropolitan vision in which we abandon the artifice of city and county. Yet I know well that such a prospect is more utopian than striking oil in your backyard.

C Richard Everett

Although coming from many different walks of life, developers seem to share a passion for what my Swedish colleague Bo Bergman poetically names 'the will to the city'. Pragmatically, Houston's 'will' is a *developmental agency* that has evolved over time while constantly reshaped by its *agents*.[12] The constituency of this agency is complex, affected by developmental constraints (as per Bob Schultz's pressure points), personal predilections and market perceptions. External agents such as competition and financing, each autonomously motivated, are augmented by personal agents – in Schultz's case perhaps stemming from his literary studies: the associated rigour of reading, its appeal to form and style and the sense of completion upon finishing a text. Like a book, a building is both a project and an object.

12. I use Marvin Minsky's distinction between 'agent' and 'agency' as explored in *The Society of Mind*, (New York: Simon and Schuster, 1986). He writes: 'I'll call "Society of Mind" this scheme in which each mind is made of smaller processes. These we'll call *agents*'. (You can build a mind from many little parts, each mindless by itself.) He continues, discussing a 'simple' machine or *Builder*: 'Let's use two different words "agent" and "agency", to say that *Builder* seems to live a double life. As agency, it seems to know its job. As agent, it cannot know anything at all'. Thus, I similarly use 'agent' to cover both Schultz's five pressure points and Schnitzers's philanthropy – neither of which know anything about the 'collective agency of development' in Houston.

In Richard Everett's case, the will to build derives from architecture degrees and from the period when, as a 'very young man', he was Shore Facilities Planning Officer for the US Navy Civil Engineer Corps stationed in Japan, and developed a taste for running things. This combination of design education and leadership might have resulted in impatience with the long and disrupted process between the architect's sketch and an occupied building. Yet as a developer he shortened the arc, if not exactly in time, then in palpable experience, since there is no lull between financing and execution in Houston: time flies when the pressure is on. And were it not for 'the city', the developer would be totally in charge. Back from Japan in 1971, Everett joined Century Development (then owned by Kenneth Schnitzer), becoming President and then CEO, and partner in Allen Center and Greenway Plaza as well as several hig- profile towers downtown, such as Wells Fargo Bank Plaza.

Schnitzer's move to densify the city in Greenway Plaza (one of the nation's first large-scale, planned urban developments emphasising extensive landscaping) may have been the signal to truly disperse and create mini-cities within the city. In 1967, he began to systematically buy up the area, for roughly $45,000 per house augmented by five years of rent-free occupancy – today an essential agent in the devel-oper's toolbox. His success may also have inspired Hines to leave the Richmond Corridor development behind and to compete by developing the Galleria just north of Greenway, which established his reputation. Schnitzer's will – as the other kingpin – was grounded in philanthropy, although it is difficult to argue over the architectural quality of the Greenway (in my view far greater than that of the Galleria). Houston's peculiar developer culture produces an ambience of professional cour-tesy, of common understanding that occasionally leads to predictable behaviours. Although no one is in charge of the non-linear city there are certain shared values based on collective experience – often as adversaries – that leads to respect for intelligence and risk taking; at least for those within the same rank of the food chain (presided over by Gerald Hines, despite his living in London). These commonalities (seen as conformity from a critical perspective) are recognisable in the similarity in form and quality between developments within each price-range, although executed by a swarm of independent developers. However, it is not wise to think of the real-estate market as a rational place – it is far from it. No mathematics will ever fully describe the gyrations of the self-organising city.

As a partner at Century Development, Everett was immersed in close encounters between kingpins and carried this experience over into the next generation of developmental agency. However, the exuberance shown by Hines and Schnitzer, and others like Dallas developer Trammel Crow (once a formidable force in the Houston market too), was severely curtailed by the energy market collapse of the early 1980s. In this sense Everett belongs to the second-generation postwar developer, buoyed by behaviours and tools of his elders, but like Frank Liu still contending with the memory of market collapse.

In 1990 Everett bought back the name 'Century Development' after Schnitzer had sold it to a Texas Savings & Loan. Essentially starting over, Everett launched Century Campus Housing Management, which became the nation's largest privatised student housing company, initiated major office projects like Reliant Energy Plaza, and performed project management services for numerous civic facilities including Hobby Center for the Performing Arts. Resurrecting a development company that had produced over 20 million square feet of space showed Everett's commitment to the company's legacy while also hedging his bets by diversifying into the national business of student housing. Yet Everett never gave up on the city. This is evident in both his civic commitment and the obvious pleasure he takes in describing Houston's new rail system or why he wanted to develop the front of 1000 Main (in the heart of downtown). For him the building is also the city. What is unique about this particular 'will to the city' is not only the development portfolio but the dedication to quality of life in the city. From the beginning Everett has spent almost half of his productive time on boards of civic organisations: Central Houston, Greater Houston Partnership, the Center for Houston's Future, the World Presidents' Organisation, the legendary Rice Center. He negates single-handedly the cliché that developers use the city for their own benefit. Everett's hero, Gerald Hines, has shown – more demonstratively and with more success than anyone else – a consistent and sustained commitment to the evolution of the city, not just the project at hand. In fact, the self-organising city would not have *any* qualities if it were not for the Princes' commitment to the surrounding context for their operations. Self-organisation does not prohibit excellence and care, although not all side effects can be foretold or forestalled.

The architectural bifurcation between vanguard commercial development and its conservative domestic counterpart (demonstrated by Gerald Hines' high-rises versus houses) can be seen in the difference between Everett's student housing and 1000 Main. Adolf Loos noted this peculiar architectural condition already in the early twentieth century when he said (and I paraphrase wildly): 'The object of art is *radical* while the art collector's house is *conservative*.' This condition will become increasingly lamentable in light of an impending energy crisis – after which all buildings, tall and

203

short, must be radically modernised, no longer as agents in the development puzzle but as a new agency with its own intelligence.

Walking around a modest office after having recently sold Century, Everett points with a sweeping gesture at an array of black and white photographs, then marches me through a portfolio of his buildings. A condensation of a 680-person office, Everett's new lair serves as a private memory palace; here, pictures are signifiers of an object lesson ambiguously distributed among dancers in the complex dance: city fathers, dwellers, real-estate lawyers, brokers, architects and the real-estate Princes whose priapic towers instigate constant turbulence along the activity surface.

Tom Forrester Lord

Born in Dallas, Lord attended the Yale Divinity School via Southern Methodist University. Upon graduation, he received an offer to work on housing legislation in Washington DC. The year was 1965. By 1967, Lord found himself working for Houston's Mayor Welch at the height of the civil rights movement. As always seems to be the case in Houston, the citizenry (bankers, home builders, real-estate professionals) urged the mayor to meet the national challenge of affordable housing – and to receive government financing through the United States Department of Housing and Urban Development (HUD). A series of committees were formed: Land Use, Housing Code and Model Cities, all motivated by the citizenry. The ambition of each committee was to find proposals that were acceptable to Washington while remaining true to the Houston spirit of free enterprise. After a long and complex process, the Land Use Committee managed to convince

HUD that deed restrictions would substitute for zoning requirements. But there was still the missing housing code. Lord had the necessary experience for this, too: after intense policy writing and political wrangling, Mayor Welch gained an audience with President Johnson, and with the support of Joseph A Califano (known in the press as 'Deputy President of Domestic Affairs'), railroaded a deal. To receive the grant, the mayor returned to Texas with the price: Houston would become the 75th Model City, after enacting a housing code. An alliance between federal government and an active and politically savvy citizenry had formed a necessary union. Isn't that what democracy is all about?

As the only real expert on housing legislation, Lord thereafter became Houston's enabler. Soon it became clear that the real problem was not building housing, but managing the 'fragile profile' of affordable housing clients. In 1971 Lord took a year off to study management at the Southwest Centre for Urban Research run by Ralph W Conant. (Conant is a firm believer in metropolitan government, which in Lord's opinion has no chance in Houston given the enormous political and economic sway held by county commissioners.) After his return Lord became one of the most respected and successful developers of affordable housing.

On one of many visits to Washington, Lord met with *New York Times* journalist John Herbers to ask why Houston was never made the national news. Herbers responded acerbically: 'Houston never fits in'.

In the end, a great enigma remains: how can a country so committed to democracy and free enterprise repeatedly marginalise Houston? Especially since initiatives are so often instigated and orchestrated by the citizenry in cooperation with (weak) local government and an occasionally strong federal government. I guess the obvious answer is that in 'normal' cities this is done through representational government, politicians and their professional staff – based on the assumption that citizens don't know what they need. NIMBYs beware…

And yet, as anthropologists of the city, how can we exclude from our vocabulary this other model – this renegade city – propelling itself at a dizzying pace along the path of our nomadic destiny?

In the meantime 'citizen amateurs' have developed two instruments to drive Houston forward – Municipal Utility Districts (MUD) for the county and Tax Increment Reinvestment Zones (TIRZ) for the city, the former creating density by spreading outwards and the latter by replacing low-density areas inside the loop. In both cases, the municipal bond serves as the essential financing instrument and subsequent tax revenues benefit the city. In fact, the astonishing financial success of TIRZ has generated revenues which now support further development – a system strangely reminiscent of a *perpetuum mobile*.

At the outer edge of developer culture, mavericks roam. The Chicago developer Sam Zell seems to have an unusual amount of risk tolerance that allows him to develop in fields that others avoid like the plague. This demonstrates the obvious point that pressure points are highly dynamic and relative. Thus, a 'professional opportunist' (as Zell describes himself) can operate amidst unusual adversity. Zell describes this as instinct, suggesting a reliance on the reptilian brain and a biology of self-organisation.[13]

13. I have a suspicion that 'instinct' is a catchphrase for an intense cooperation between the reptilian brain and the frontal lobe, allowing logic, vision and instinct to appear under a synthetic and slightly illusive label. Incidentally, Zell has made headlines lately because of his purchase of a major Chicago newspaper, now in receivership, prompting the reaction: 'Shoemaker, stay with your last!' See Collin Levy, 'Professor Risk', The Wall Street Journal, 20–21 October 2007.

Subdivision (cul-de-sac under construction)

Managing Self-Organisation

John Mixon's eyes sparkle when he refers to the conclusion of his paper (co-authored by McGlynn), 'A New Zoning and Planning Metaphor', in which they suggest that what the city needs is a *management component* to resolve conflicts between what are considered incompatible uses. His glee is enhanced by an 'I told you so' from his zoning argument in the 1993 election (when zoning advocates lost for a third time): 'If we had zoning this would never happen' – referring to the self-organised neighbourhood group who protested vigorously (and successfully) to stop the introduction of a high-rise building in a predominantly residential district [briefly described earlier in the chapter]. Mixon continues: 'and it is particularly ironic, since many of the surrounding inhabitants probably voted against zoning in 1993'. In hindsight, I should have told him that self-organisation works! Yet Mixon's concern is more complex, he has deep philosophical problems with so-called spot-zoning that would be applied in a traditionally zoned city in this case. He prefers a more flexible and dynamic system of judgement steered by continuously changing land use patterns in cities such as Houston.

Mixon and McGlynn argue that modern communications enable us to leave behind the static 'utopian land use planning' of the past with its untenable links between static comprehensive plans and spot-zoning, in favour of a planning system based on the state of land use in the current situation. In short, the authors argue that planning is relevant but must be more agile: seeking a balance between various interests in order to tame more rampant entrepreneurial instincts. In other words, M&M want to inch closer to the reality of the entrepreneurial city but still create balance. A question remains: is this 'managing' or (more provocatively) 'meddling' compatible with a self-organising system? And more fundamentally, why 'balance' if the system thrives on imbalance? Especially since there is among the swarm of developers an unwritten code of conduct that swallows imbalance, allowing the 'losers' to move on. Stephen Fox would argue that such conduct is a reflection of the Southern Protestant ethic that by some obscure process has trickled down into the development community. Would it be possible to evolve this ethic to such a degree that conflicts might be fewer and further between? Or is 'conflict' a pseudo-problem hiding the more sinister consequences of self-organisation?

M&M suggest a set of instruments for an 'Informative Comprehensive Plan'. These instruments would indirectly manage the complex system by providing dynamic information and relying on the latest interactive computer technology. This would allow citizens and developers alike to observe in detail the underlying premises of a project; both opportunities and constraints. As such, the instruments would form the backdrop against which land planning decisions would be made – all in the name of striking a balance. The early steps (paraphrased):[14]

a zoomable map of the subject area, accessed via the internet by search engines such as Google Earth

an edited overlay map displaying highways, streets and waterways

an environmental assessment report

a map displaying all current land uses

14. Mixon and McGlynn, op cit.

a display of current tax values and building permits

maps displaying projected time-sequenced changes that reveal future investments in public amenities by all government entities

the provision of interactive capabilities to allow the exploration of various 'if-then' scenarios by networking all agencies to permit instant updating

making these instruments available to anyone interested

Currently this type of information is considered 'proprietary knowledge' held close to the chest and at varying degrees by each developer. Resistance, particularly among those who consider themselves 'in the know', will probably be met with attempts to make this information available to anyone interested, since it may allow more 'amateurs' to enter the game. Pulling the playing field out of its current obscurity may greatly increase the opportunity for environmental health by allowing those concerned with environmental stewardship early insight. Similarly, it would bring into focus the developer's responsibility to the health and well-being of the citizenry – suggesting that the altruism which comes late in a productive life should in fact accompany the developer throughout his or her career. M&M puts this shrewdly and diplomatically:

Not least of all, an information-based planning process responds sensitively to the new science. It authorises a degree of chaos to keep the system stable. It eliminates the rigidity of adopted plans. It allows land uses and regulations to emerge. And it allows anyone, including idle observers, to see emergence in action as the land use patterns work themselves out through the years, responding immediately to the strong, weak and strange attractors that can be managed, but not anticipated nor strictly controlled.

But nagging questions do remain: what does authorising 'a degree of chaos' mean? And how exactly, in the end, can attractors be managed? I am assuming that relative flexibility is limited by a supervisory agency – a city arbitration unit attached to the legislative body, and when this fails, the courts. But what about the implication that knowing more will increase the sense of responsibility among developers and citizens alike – is this just my own naïveté?

These questions will remain unanswered for a time, since there is still much to learn about self-organisation. Optimistically, I have a vision in mind of a mature self-organising city, far beyond its current adolescence, with a dramatic effect motivated by the maturation of its collective mind. In other words: a city with an internal control system in no need of outside regulation – a terribly exciting premise for this boundless prairie.

The Workings of the Middle Landscape: Biological Versus Mechanical Analogies

For too long we have considered cities best organised by external command, as machines for living, designed entirely by human intention. Yet so many modern cities, particularly the sprawling kind, seem to develop without apparent oversight, through spontaneous human interventions. These differ radically from the edicts, plans, legislation, regulations and templates that comprise traditional instruments of planning. By contrast, the actions of developers are dynamically adjusted, redirected, changed, abandoned and fine-tuned in response to both positive and negative feedback.[15]

When land prices become too high developers withdraw, often leapfrogging to find greener pastures. This type of negative feedback is used in biological systems 'to stabilise physiological processes': reaching for a sweater when it becomes too cold, or shivering.[16] Leapfrogging as escape tactic and risk aversion is a dominant negative feedback system in Houston. It must be taken seriously as an (often) overlooked prime mover in this particular city's self-organisation. Clearly this is how the field expands – in leaps and bounds – leaving large lacunae in its wake.

As described earlier in the chapter, whenever developer Frank Liu introduced an attractor into a weak field, the reaction among smaller developers – whose major tool is mimicry – was to follow suit. They react like a school of pilot fish that swarm around a shark (or ship) to pick up stray morsels after the big feed: ectoparasites amongst fish, small shrimp amongst developers.[17] New development reverses the negativity of leapfrogging; here the turbulence is positive – an economics of love versus fear. Just as fishy behaviour is constrained by ocean currents, depth, visibility and water temperature, besides the internal constraints of developer behaviour there exist 'templates' in the form of infrastructure

15. Norbert Wiener, the father of cybernetics, included self-organisation in his interest in communication and control 'in animal and machine'. In this sense, cybernetics may be the meta-concept of such urbanisation, since it includes digital, mechanical and biological communication and control systems.

16. Scott Camazine et al., *Self-Organisation in Biological Systems.* (Princeton, NJ and Oxford: Princeton University Press, 2001), 15.

17. William N. Eschmeyer and Earl Stannard Herald, *A Field Guide to Pacific Coast Fishes: North America* (1983), Peterson Field Guides (New York: Houghton Mifflin, 1999), 208.

and a formidable bundle including finance and building regulations, market perception and technology that circumscribe behaviour in Liu's domain.

Inside this field there is a measure of liberty and openness that allows the developer to perform a peculiarly synchronised dance, not unlike fireflies which mysteriously activate their 'lights' one after another, so that it is difficult to separate the dancers from the dance. In fact, there is no leader who begins flashing the abdominal lantern, but rather a type of communal mimesis. 'Incident lighting', the general awareness of light on all bodies, speeds up the synchronous and rhythmic flashing.[18]

This is particularly relevant to mimickers who hover over the field, ready to rush in when an attractor starts to blow. The smaller developers also require an external catalyst – the arrival of springtime – which sets the stage for the mating impulse to kick in, thus making the fireflies flash. Mimickers don't communicate with each other, but like the wreckers swarming a traffic accident, they 'know' when to dance.

Whether developers construct major attractors or simply mimic other developers, an internal control system is involved. It is hard to make the case that particular types of developers are as graceful as schools of fish 'moving cohesively, almost in unison, as flawlessly as if they were part of a single organism'.[19] Yet within the pattern we mistakenly perceive as disorganised sprawl, consistency and uniformity strongly suggest that developer behaviour is indeed a form of schooling, in the sense that they ascribe to the same 'school' and that they school like fish within the communication and control system.

Recall Bob Schultz's list of pressure points and assume for a moment that all proactive developers share these concerns to a greater or lesser degree. When a developer is let loose in an

18. Scott Camazine et al, op cit, 149–50.
19. Ibid, 167.

open or weak field we see again and again how a menu of evasive manoeuvres are performed to avoid the 'pressures' and reach the prey. These formations are clearly not as elegant as either 'flash expansion' or the 'fountain effect' among fish, yet the resulting land graphic of a suburban subdivision, viewed from above, is simply beautiful.[20]

The precursory manoeuvres that underlie these graphics may be similar to what biologists call the Trafalgar effect – a type of formation suggesting that developers of large attractors 'communicate' with the same rapid battlefield signals that Nelson's fleet of ships used at Trafalgar, now operating in time, not necessarily in the same space.[21] These collective motions produce repeated patterns of both cause and effect.

Biologists surely would baulk at these analogies, just as planners would criticise the recklessness suggested by such dynamic behaviours.

But the peculiar dance performed in Houston suggests that it is time to rethink the hopelessly inadequate model of the city as a machine. Our challenge is to recognise that cities are neither machines nor organic systems but simultaneously both – fusing the technological and the natural in such a way as to require a new science. Viewed in this light, Houston is no longer bizarre, but presents itself as a laboratory for renewed understanding – an opportunity to grasp the organic dimension of cities and their systemic logic that operates from the general premise of 'a single-family house sitting in a subdivision' as its most basic unit that (together with its accoutrements, from freeways to schools) in 'leaps and bounds' fills in, and out, the endless field. Simplicity becomes complexity. The whole is more than its parts.

20. Ibid, 174.
21. Ibid, 167.

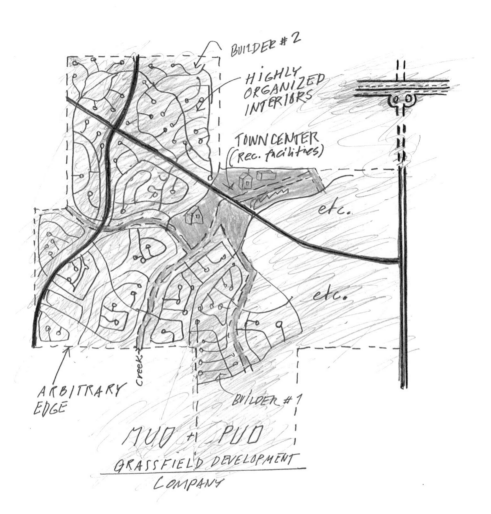

BUILDER #2

HIGHLY
ORGANIZED
INTERIORS

TOWN CENTER
(Rec. facilities)

etc.

etc.

ARBITRARY
EDGE

Creek

BUILDER #1

MUD + PUD
GRASSFIELD DEVELOPMENT
COMPANY

Subdivisions

Home on the Prairie

While incessant movement holds urbanites in its orbit, the suburban life they may have known is changing. Once you enter the westward trajectory and step onto the carousel – the turbulence caused by strange attractors, regardless of size and magnitude – life on the prairie is all-absorbing. Is it unreasonable to see this pull and concomitant turbulence as the logical evolution of that original 'errand into the wilderness', with its stubborn clearing of indigenous forest?[1] Here in the determined breach in the vast wilderness, a dream is born. The city is but an obfuscation of Manifest Destiny, the great leap across the continent is the real drive forward. But another competing desire encumbers this leap: the dream of the perfect community, best illustrated by the perils of a 'city upon the hill'. This complex amalgamation is American distance, the internalised struggle between community and freedom that shapes our outward spatial conceptions. These are the movements that make the attenuated city possible. Only under the influence of westward movement and turbulence can future transformations be projected. The inertia of these forces is continually underestimated in favour of viewing suburban life as mere lifestyle, predictable and essentially static. But 'home on the prairie' will always be characterised by restlessness and change. In 2009, California, the western *locus solus* of the American Dream, along with its storied cities of San Francisco and Los Angeles, are nearing bankruptcy. But it would be a mistake to think the fall of the most glamorous state in the union signals the end of the American Dream.

Precisely because of the inadequacy of previous concepts of suburbia, and lately of the metropolis, cities like Houston,

1. Perry Miller, *Errand into the Wilderness*
(Cambridge, MA: Harvard University Press, 1956).

Phoenix, Orlando and others must find more descriptive nomenclature. For Houston I have settled on 'the middle landscape' (or more poetically 'the city of a third kind'), although it does not exist in the minds of its inhabitants. Their view is a privileged, selective and vaguely conceptual one: 'I live in Houston', upon further questioning, is rapidly narrowed down to a personal world limited by everyday activities. Understood by a few as an ecological footprint, there are as many versions of these footfalls as there are ambulatory inhabitants. Houston, the open city, provides this generosity. But precisely because of the ecological question in its broadest sense, we must ask ourselves how a 'middle landscape' might help us to rethink the personalised haven of diffuse human occupation. We begin by turning to everyday life.

Double Space

Physical space, the most fundamental horizon of human habitat, has changed tremendously over the last century. While material surroundings remain relatively stable, Houstonians have radically altered their speed whilst rapidly expanding their field of action, obscuring and altering perception of the setting. The suburban city, much more than the traditional city, is the product of this dramatic spatial expansion. Add to this the emergence of virtual space and a new spatial domain appears.

This space is far removed from the Spanish plazas that stunned me when I first travelled to Barcelona in the early 1960s, and from the many cathedrals that I have lingered in during hot afternoons in many other Mediterranean cities. Nolli's 1748 map of Rome summarises this space well. Encountering the Pantheon in that city I hypothesised the first version of *double space*, characterised by the dimly lit occupiable space that the French call *pochée* – roughly, pocketed space – inserted between the inner and outer shells which enclose it. The central space surrounds the viewer, who stands transfixed, then climbs along the inside shell to literally perform space. In this sliver of space, trajectory replaces contemplation, foreshadowing the next generation of double space.

Two metropolitan speeds have propelled two new types of spatiality: the first is the dizzying pace of the freeway. The transfixed subject held in place by awe in the temple has become permanently displaced, a hurtling projectile. The driver carves space into megashapes and incessant patterns that flicker in filmic panorama.

Second is a new galaxy of virtual space emanating from an array of devices: radios, TVs, telephones and handhelds, which create, expand and foreshorten distances previously confined to the imaginary.

The two spaces – actual and virtual – equally resist fixity. Although enfolded and embedded, they remain clearly separate. This new double space, of which we can only see the vague outlines, is both the projected physical envelope surrounding me as I career along the highway (or settle into the subdivision's somnambulant pace) and the virtual space defined by incomprehensible warp-speeds – a new Piranesian space that will never be fully known. One open space only half imagined, the other racing at the outer edge of my peripheral vision: both are forever emerging, no longer anchored by the built but sketched by new ephemeral – yet real – lines, points and fields of power. The new double space has finally undone the claustrophobia of a nation of cul-de-sacs.

Why is suburbia the locus of such a peculiar revolution? Leaving the city behind, the new suburbanites are overwhelmed by decisions (to move) and all-absorbing activities (child-rearing). In time it becomes obvious that what was left behind in the city is never replaced. In this perfect vacuum, imagination and technological revolution prosper. Is it entirely surprising that so much virtuality emerges in Silicon Valley, itself a vast suburb? The suburban garage – that unglamorous resting place for so much horsepower – clearly desires something more. *Horror vacui*. The second space, loosely attached to the edge of the cul-de-sac, compensates for its finitude by providing an unknowable, wide-open space that is ever expanding. Under the auspices of a giant 'server cloud', constructed virtual worlds swarm with avatars.

The virtual orchestrates a new type of space populated by communities with an arsenal of new propinquities, transforming the seemingly endless digital realm into new conurbations; some gated, some occupied by the like-minded. In time, these villages become global villages: the glorious evolution of *homo suburbanus*.

Fundamentally, this hyperspace affects our sense of distance and time, which may suggest new environmental design. Will the need to physically travel decline, reducing cravings for distance? Will this lead to a denser city, actually more gated while virtually completely open? Would this be 'a genuine step forward into a new psychological realm', since the peculiar openness associated with electronic communication may construct new intimacy and new forms of community? Will the result be more generic environments, mere consoles for communication? But then there is the body – the seamless extension of the highly elastic human brain – and its beyond: the environment that we can no longer keep at arm's length.

At this point the two spaces are discrete. Will a time come when we can no longer distinguish one from the other? There is potential for a new spatial vista, where we might project a new world, ever closer to our fertile imagination. An insistent simultaneity in which the real and the virtual appear side by side or cut into one another the way a TV programme cuts into everyday life, but now more invasively; only action restores the difference and gives shape to reality.

Divided City

For the time being, we have to cope with double space, each sphere operating at its own pace (among other bifurcations). Those concerned with its planning and development must contend with two Houstons, a city and a county, one presumably urban and the other suburban. Yet it is a conceptual division I studiously avoid since the pavilion – the fundamental suburban building type – is the dominant type in the entire region. This freestanding object is *surrounded* by open space, unlike the atrium *surrounding* an open space. Houston, if anything, is simply *suburban*. Furthermore, the false opposition between city and county conceals the few occasions when the city pattern is too close to the suburban pattern to be considered a distinct zone within Houston city limits. The bifurcation is a complete misnomer because upon closer scrutiny, there are four patterns: urban, suburban, rural and tracts of empty land – all intermixed – comfortably contained within the vast field. This alphabet soup does not fit a sharp duality. Considering both sparsely and unoccupied land suggests a radical shift in *boundaries*, lifting the view of the entire settlement far above current myopic levels. The city–county divide refuses Houston's seamless geographical contiguity and morphological diversity; similarities between the two are more important than differences. Not to speak of the disastrous consequences of a divided power structure

Divided City (Harris County and the City of Houston)

(the city mayor and county judge) lamented by developers. The outer zones of the county appear to self-organise more than the inner city, where a powerful mayor interferes too frequently and too aggressively, with good intentions (and within the powers invested in the office) but not in the interests of self-organisation. City lore has it that one mayor (Lanier) loved to pour concrete and so he pushed freeways and parking tarmacs, another (Brown) believed in public transportation but managed only to implement a short link between TMC and downtown, whereas the last mayor (White) has a keen affection for solving 'urgent problems' like freeway congestion and access to pocket parks – indicating that each mayor instinctively trusted self-organisation by concentrating on the public dimension of the city. Yet micro-scale mayoral decisions – the daily thumbs-up or -down – exercise a considerable warping effect on self-organisation. In my limited understanding of their achievements, no mayor has dealt seriously or consistently with daunting environmental problems. For example, flooding has been regarded not as an 'environmental problem caused by development' but as a problem *for* development – and for those living on the flood plane. The metropolitan field has a working smoothness expressed by leapfrogging and the resultant holey plane. Despite causing considerable change, and often damage, the geographical openness of the field and the behaviour of metropolitan community agents (from developers to regulators to architects to financiers to citizens) allow its development to continue. They are engaged in a spontaneous yet coherent metropolitan dance – not unlike fireflies on a summer night. Though there is an appearance of orchestration, in fact no single human intention runs the show.

An uninterrupted view of the middle landscape flattens and widens the perspective of the bisected city. But once the dazzling range of virtual communications are written in, a new world appears: if not the world, the nation; now a vast metropolitan world roughly bookended by the Pacific, the Rockies and the great New England megalopolis.

The Post-Geographic Middle Landscape

Returning by car from Donald Judd's Marfa a decade ago, I first got an inkling of the collapse of the city's boundary. The seven-hour road trip becomes a commute thanks to the radio programme originating in Houston, never allowing me to lose contact. Another trip to Larry McMurtry's Archer City, where one million books cast a spell the size of a major weather system, and I realise that the dove is no longer so lonesome. Metropolitan flyways have inadvertently exploded the city. Marfa is within Houston's conceptual reach, as much as the nearby oilfields in Midland. Archer City is a peculiar town-as-bookstore on the outskirts of the Dallas–Fort Worth metro-plex. Today traditional city boundaries are more akin to the nets of trawlers that greedily enclose more and more of their catch. Even agriculture has become urban, its tractors piped with satellite radio, telecommunications and air-conditioning – no one is far out of reach in the middle landscape. A huge elastic power-field, urbanity is no longer defined by geography even if stretching to drilling-platforms far out in the Gulf of Mexico, because it is also raised up along air- and radio-waves in the ephemeral dominion of electronics and psychology.[2] The next generation of Houstonians must break decisively with the divided city, to view Houston as non-geographic entity shrinking and expanding in imaginative ways within an emerging middle landscape.

Yet to realise that we have left behind the geographic, or more precisely adjusted its importance in the metropolitan network society, requires us to alter our worldview. Suburbia is no longer isolated, it is both very much here and nowhere; after all, emails have essentially no geographical point of origin although they (no longer very) secretly do, and roadrunners calling from mobile telephones are 'out of pocket' (at least for now). Suburbia is no longer a bastion of alienation and ennui. Metropolitan ailments (and metropolitan happiness) are now distributed evenly across the entire field, regardless of patterns of habitation. Although environmentally challenged, Houston's leapfrogged spaces – fragmented remainders of prairie – may be the only spaces without human problems (unless you happen to step into a nest of fire ants). The remaining global challenge is to distribute opportunity in this vague terrain.[3] Increasingly, concerned citizens and groups have become aware of mounting environmental problems, yet they have yet to elect 'their' mayor. Organisations such as *Trees for Houston* have become de facto custodians of the vulnerable zoohemic canopy, while the Gulf Coast Institute under David Crossley is concerned with much wider issues:

The Gulf Coast Institute seeks a liveable community with a dynamic economy that revitalises and protects

2. In a course outline, Kazys Varnelis describes cities as networks: '*Network City explores how key urban areas have developed as ecosystems of competing networks. Networks of capital, transportation infrastructure and telecommunications systems have simultaneously centralised cities while dispersing them into larger post-urban fields such as the Northeastern seaboard or Southern California. Linked together through networks, such cities form the core of global capital, producing the geography of flows that structures economies and societies today.*' [As is too often the case among us urbanists, Varnelis uses a beguiling analogical description that, if not carefully explored, leaves us with only that.]

3. Ignasi Solà-Morales, the Catalan architect and critic, seemed to be the first to have used the French term in the English-language press when he asked himself: *What is to be done with these enormous voids, with their imprecise limits and vague definition? Art's reaction is to preserve these alternative, strange spaces. Architecture's destiny has always been colonisation, the imposing of limits, order and form, the introduction into strange space of the elements of identity necessary to make it recognisable, identical, universal.* 'Terrain Vague', *Anyplace*, ed Cynthia Davidson (Cambridge, MA: MIT Press, 1995), 119.

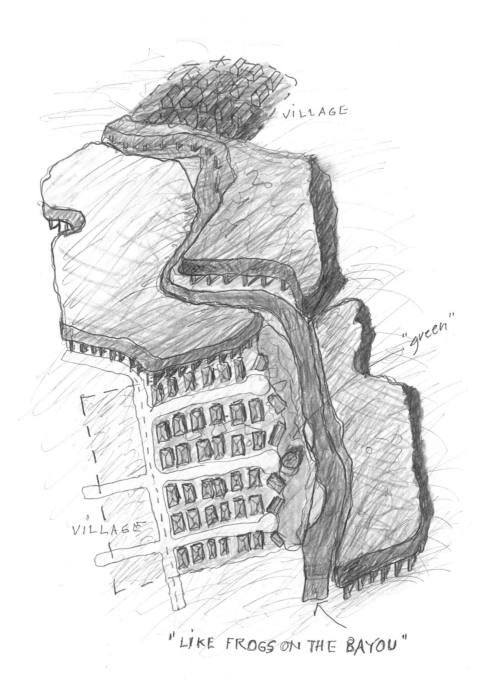

'Like Frogs around the Bayous'

neighbourhoods, improves access, increases mobility choices, improves air and water quality, protects green space and natural resources and builds a sense of place and community.

At least two metropolitan cultures exist: one described above by the Gulf Coast Institute's mission statement and the other demonstrated by the electorate's three-time rejection of zoning legislation. The worldview of these no-zoners is embedded in American distance: 'I want to get around as easily as possible, but I don't want to live too close to anyone. Since I have to, I want to live close to people like me.' The basic ethos of this probably large majority is the American Dream of 'living in my own house' and Houston, more than any metropolis, provides single-family houses in the $100,000 range – a rarity in the national housing market, at least before the current collapse. In economic terms, Houston may be the most democratic city in the union.

'Like frogs around the bayous'

The small but active group of 'progressives' and the large majority are worlds apart. While progressives see the need for a radical reorganisation of housing, by increasing density near freeways to shorten commuting distances and thereby de-emphasise single-family housing, the others strive not to give up on the original desire to live in the suburbs. The difference between these collective, opposing, ambitions is fundamental. The majority is neither homogenous nor easily distinguished by economic criteria – both the upper- and the lower-middle classes nurture similar desires; this is directly reflected by the representatives serving in all levels of government. It behoves those of us who see the urgency for change to pay close attention to this reality and to find a way to make use of the predominant development model in the city, its self-organisation. Change comes from within, at the very centre of the neighbourhood, driven by an increasingly concerned public. According to Steven Klineberg's yearly studies of public opinion, an awareness is emerging that collective action may be necessary not only to preserve, but to improve the suburban dream. Patience and attention.

The middle landscape is going through a subtle but insistent transformation. The change is a double action: first, the persistent decentralisation of everything from housing to services (what we normally refer to as sprawl) and second, consolidation of the dispersal. As if a giant first spread out his arms to smooth out the built material, and then gathered it back together into smaller heaps. Yet it is an organisational change, not necessarily physical. With the boundary of urbanisation pushed to the horizon, now everything is urbanised, everything regional. Wilderness, however vast and majestic, has become parkland in a giant metropolitan region. All farming is urban farming. Watching the steady back-and-forth of helicopters clipping above a Galveston beach, black spots against the morning sun, brings to mind that oil-workers, too, are metropolitan commuters circulating from the centre to the outer edges.

In Houston, sprawl-shaping has taken place since the beginning. Atomisation, no longer solely along ethnic lines (although that happens too) is primarily based on economic and cultural similarities; put more pragmatically, to protect real-estate values. Traditionally, social striations in Houston have been among four ethnic sectors (black, white, Hispanic, Vietnamese) but due to the growth of the middle class, which operates outside ethnic lines, the stratification is increasingly fine-tuned. An *archipelago* of communities is emerging – islands of order – physically in terms of typical subdivision layout and socially cohesive in 'towns and villages'. It is modern tribalisation quite different to the urban renewal of the 1960s when both feds and the city government tried, as it turned out desperately, to construct community anew. In Houston NIMBY actions have matured from occasional citizen revolts against development into an impetus for serious neighbourhood organisation – the new choice tool in the self-organising metropolis, now in the hands of its citizenry. Although the effectiveness of citizen action is in direct proportion to income – the richer the neighbourhood the greater organisational strength – a metropolitan community of villages is in the making. Just as Plato described the 1,500 city-states surrounding the Aegean Sea as 'frogs around a pond', so do the hundreds of loosely formed neighbourhoods and some 120 incorporated cities of Houston sit 'like frogs around the bayous'. Could this be the return of grass-roots democracy?

In the end, Athens rounded everything and everyone up into one city-state (with the help of capital from silver mining), while in contemporary America the frogs are only croaking to signal their presence. The increasing inability of Congress to act, coupled with the desire for self-determination at both city and state levels, forces individuals to realise that they had better organise and take action, in some cases, because nobody else is doing so, though in Houston this is standard behaviour, and not only among developers ('That's why we voted against zoning!'). Tocqueville sensed the inclination to act locally as an innate American desire when he warned against centralised government – the tyranny of the majority.

Front Yard Democracy

We must return to the scene of self-organisation visited in the last chapter, now from a different perspective.

Driving through an upscale district inside the loop, an observer cannot help noticing that aside from the usual gaudy electrical decorations anticipating the holidays, some unusual messages grace front lawns. Reacting to the unwanted intrusion of an impending high-rise building, a spontaneous neighbourhood emerges demonstratively in the form of hundreds of bright yellow signs decrying the 'Tower of Traffic'. The self-organised neighbourhood coalition has inadvertently *mapped* itself, like some ancient tribe applying war paint to prepare for battle. The demonstration instantly reveals an existing subdivision organisation headed by activists with phone and email lists ready, and rooted in the yearly 4 July party or occasional meeting. Common interests and culture, formed in suburban backyards and around barbecue pits, pools and basketball hoops is now confirmed in the front yard. Solidarity cemented by a specific set of deed restrictions, together with political vigilance, shifts power from the city to its citizens.

The organisation in Braeburn Valley just outside the inner loop does not flaunt its colours, although it remains as vigilant as any other neighbourhood coalition. As often seems to be the case there is one person – the activist – who establishes direct access to the local police and even a live video surveillance camera keeping watch for the illegal or merely unusual. Held in place by deed restrictions and armed with an effective information system, the activist keeps an eye on everyday life as well as 'the big condo project' across the way. Recently, she gathered her forces to face a high-rise building threat, but needlessly, as the developer withdrew of his own volition. Through police connections, neighbourhoods can form pseudo-cities within cities, always around the same set of concerns. A political advertisement for an aspiring city council member captures the mood of these cities-within-cities. The candidate's priorities are to:

Serve the taxpayers, not the special interests

Increase police protection and public safety

Improve flood control

Work with neighbourhoods to prevent unwanted development

Preserve the character of our neighbourhoods

(The candidate is also a husband, a father of three children and a business owner.) The ideology is transparent: defend the turf, fight crime,[4] keep floodwater out, organise NIMBY action if needed, maintain property values, defend the right of families to live in single-family houses (and by the way) support small business: 'Our neighbourhoods are what makes this city great'. The desire to build fences around each neighbourhood may be a way to 'circle the wagons' in the face of *terrain vague* – to cope with the endless metropolitan expanse. We can safely assume that this slow but insistent reorganisation is the future of the middle landscape.

The radically different worldviews of the progressives and

4. Although crime is a reality in all American cities, in Houston serious crime coincides with poverty and is therefore of secondary concern in this particular inner city neighbourhood, but still an essential aspect of the ideology of gated communities. Gating takes at least two forms: walls, gates, guards, dogs and guns more common in the outer, upper-middle-class suburbs, while in the inner city, security guards often patrol the neighbourhood in marked cars.

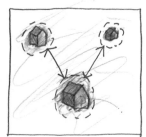

COMMUNITY
WITHOUT
PROPINQUITY

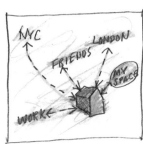

VIRTUAL
COMMUNITY

NIMBY COMMUNITY
(UNDER STRESS)

Communities

the new Urban Villagers – the former committed to the planned city and the latter to the open city, remain in seemingly hopeless opposition. How is an ideological conflict of this magnitude resolved? How long can the progressives' quixotic struggle continue, and how long can the majority live oblivious to the side effects of its habits? To paraphrase Norman Mailer: 'the metropolis is a persuasion of architectural skulls in search of a brain'. The formation of such a brain lies in a coalition in which the progressive's global understanding and commitment is joined with the villager's dreams and aspirations. When the neighbourhood activists add metropolitan vigilance to their list of concerns, Houston will change.

Metropolitan regions like Houston, in the past largely in the hands of developers, their cohorts in government and docile consumers, are seeing their citizens awaken after the dawn of the NIMBYs. This, in turn, will increase the pressure to elaborate devices such as deed restrictions and expand the menus of municipal utility districts into elaborate eco-domains. As always, the most formidable obstacle to a true suburban revolution is cost. The discrepancy between what citizens would like and what they are willing to pay for is always wide. Only education and thorough understanding by all parties will narrow the gap between dollars and dreams. Yet there are new opportunities, as the German philosopher Peter Sloterdijk writes:

> The turn to the province can also be a turn to real macro-history that more closely attends to the regulation of life in the framework of nature, agriculture and ecology than all previous industrial world images could... Reduced to short formulas, the city is not the fulfilment of existence; nor are the goals of industrial capitalism; nor scientific progress;

nor more civilization, more cinema, more home beautiful, longer vacations, better eating: none of these things is the fulfilment of existence. What is 'authentic' will always be something else. You must know who you are.[5]

Will *homo suburbanus* have a better chance to achieve authenticity than the beleaguered *homo urbanus* surrounded, in Sloterdijk's words, by the culture of 'distraction, talk, curiosity, un-housedness, habitualness … homelessness, fear, being unto-death'? This seems unlikely, unless the impoverished conception of space that has and still dominates the subdivision is transformed. Its goal must be the ambition to *produce human beings* that Sloterdijk provocatively sees as the fundamental role of space.[6] But as suggested by his nine dimensions of anthropological space, such an endeavour is very complex and demanding. He writes:

> I describe the human-generating island [substitute: subdivision] as a nine-dimensional space in which each of the dimensions must exist for the human-generating effect to be triggered. If only one dimension is absent, you do not get a complete human. It all starts with the chirotrope, the place of the hand. And what does the hand have to do with the genesis of the human? The answer to this question provides a first version of a theory of action, an elementary pragmatics. I then tackle the phonotope, the space of sound in which groups that hears themselves [sic] tarry. Then this is followed by the uterotope, the space occupied by deeper-seated memberships of shared caves; the thermotope, the sphere of warmth or the space where you

5. Peter Sloterdijk, *Critique of Cynical Reason*, Theory and History of Literature vol 40 (Minneapolis, MN: University of Minnesota Press, 1987), 205.

6. Peter Sloterdijk, 'Spheres Theory: Talking to Myself About the Poetics of Space', *Harvard Design Magazine* 30, Spring/Summer 2009, 131–33.

get spoiled; and the erototope, the place of jealousy and the field of desire … the ergotope, the field of war and effort; the thanotope, the space of coexistence with the dead in which religious symbols prevail and finally the nomotope, the space of legal tensions that provide the group with a normative backbone.[7]

Although one -tope appears missing from the list of eight above (is it the original architectural tope, the ancient structure, in the form of a dome or tumulus that in Sanskrit is known as the *thupe*?), we can sense how the typical subdivision, with its cookie-cutter houses planted gracefully on their own lots along a curving street, might appear crude and unevolved. Yet we also know that the beginnings, or better the *remnants* of his topes hover in house and lot as ghosts of a world that could have been, if only the 'architects of suburbia' had seen the subdivision as the first experiment of a greater project.

But the doubling of the spatial dimension, giving depth and resonance to the phonotope (and several other -topes) suggests that life at the end of the cul-de-sac has reached its nadir. To thicken the human plot we must add new dimensions. The elevation of architectural space to anthropological space further implies that architects can have a second life designing beyond a pretty facade.

7. Ibid, 131–32.

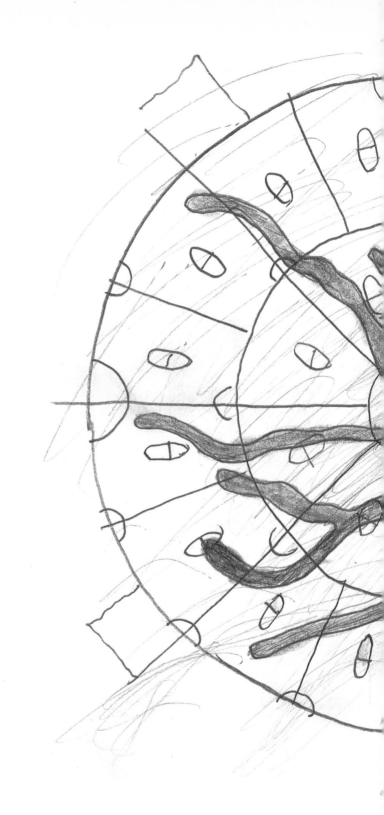

Obstacles and Opportu-
nities

The holey plane, the most graphic expression of the diffuse middle landscape, is studded with pregnant voids – actual and virtual – of loss and opportunity. One such conceptual hole, with direct practical consequences, is best illustrated by Ralph Ellifrit's diagram of 1948, which reveals in astonishing graphic clarity that only the *artificial* is in focus for the suburban planner of the late 1940s. Nature is taken for granted or simply forgotten. Nature's absence from the equation seems particularly perplexing since Houston, beyond manifesting the edenic American Dream, is a decisive encounter with weather: heat and humidity; and the vagaries of the moist prairie: flooding and gumbo soil. This wildness is and will remain an obstacle. So why is the moist prairie demonstratively ignored? Is it because Houston's dream originated from further east? As Gaston Bachelard wrote, 'We bring our lairs with us.'

Fifty years later, the prairie is acknowledged, but always corrected or subjugated. Nature is still a stage set. (And the leaf-blower ultimate symbol of this absurd contradiction.) Ellifrit's neglect is understandable – after all, he only drew a diagram. But he might have been smarter to leave it blank, as degree zero, because of its magnificent availability. Now graphically expressed as holes, the careless rips and tears in the built fabric result from the leapfrogging development patterns discussed earlier. No wonder that the conceptual vacuum is now filled with the vengeance of renewed environmentalism. Today this string of lacunae forms a conceptual and actual centre.

Environmental concerns have existed in Houston since the 1930s, although restricted to a small elite and some enlightened city officials. Only in the last decade has pollution of various kinds come to the attention of the average citizen. That attaining what is vaguely called 'sustainability' is an enormously costly and daunting task has yet to sink in. Eisenhower's

241

highway programme pales in comparison. Strategic thinking on a regional and national scale is required, entirely foreign middle landscape pragmatics driven by the self-interest of builders and occupants. Furthermore, the major problem in American urbanism is not new growth, but what to do about the existing stock of highly inefficient buildings and transportation systems. I think of the solution to this predicament as the Giant Retro-Fit. Literally an air-conditioned nightmare, outdated buildings are now recognised by federal research organisations such as the National Science Foundation, Department of Energy and the Environmental Protection Agency in their call for engineering sustainable buildings.[1]

Yet the call for sustainability is utterly bewildering. On the diffuse plains of the middle landscape, the concept is not only vague but seen as plagued by ideology and self-righteousness, particularly amongst agents of daily change. Although the tide is shifting among denizens, achieving a public informed by the complexity and expense of the task is a long and arduous process. The American public has never been willing to face the true environmental costs of development. Not to mention that the transition from understanding to electing the right politicians to alter behaviours among agents of change is rife with obstacles. In Houston, a city dominated by individual concerns and only incidentally by the public good, the change needed is truly radical. Only a programme closely tied to economic incentives for the construction industry and quality of life for occupants will do. I would also argue that such a programme must also be pragmatic, providing actual built examples of public good – similar in scope to the federal highway programme. Yet the programme should ideally

1. *Science in Energy and Environmental Design (SEED): Engineering Sustainable Buildings* www.nsf.gov/pubs/2009/nsf09606/nsf09606.htm

spring from the field itself, administered and steered by a coalition of residents, local government and most importantly, the development community. A utopian team effort that is difficult to imagine.

One of my favourite mediators, JB Jackson, wrote elegantly (10 years after Ellifrit's diagram): 'So the job of the urbanist and architect is essentially to design a man-made environment *which is as natural as possible*'.[2] Jackson, in 1959, understands fully that the dichotomous way of thinking of man and environment as totally separate has come to an end. In his view it is time to rethink. But he is also a pragmatist who sees with his own eyes, on forays with his motorbike, that America is a country *in the making* – forever on the road to completion. Thus he suggests we should design as 'natural as possible', strategically confined by what is achievable – the opposite of the clearly unattainable notion of 'sustainability' (a frictionless *perpetuum mobile*). Its fundamental vagueness shrouded in moral overtones, sustainability will always undermine our confidence: there is no way to know with certainty what is sustainable, while Jackson seems to suggest that we will know in our hearts whether we have done our best.

As Natural As Possible

Spring 2008. Across the middle landscape, I see our winter slowly heading north and the zoohemic canopy beginning to green. The forest of solar pumps is enriching the region by hinting at the symbiotic relationship between trees, prairie and bayou. Below my window, the old stables, the last of the

2. John Brinckerhoff Jackson, *Landscapes: Selected Writings by JB Jackson*, ed Erwin H Zube (Amherst, MA: University of Massachusetts Press, 1970), 79.

agricultural landscape, have been replaced by adjacent white-collar prisons. Fifty years after JB Jackson's suggestion that 'man belongs to nature' we are still in severe denial. In the blogosphere, a public raves about impending environmental disaster, from rising waters to roving clouds of distemper. But the bizarre contradiction between the real and the virtual demonstrates that we still operate in two very different spaces. Is the invention of the virtual world just another escape? Now an escape from suburbia, the worldwide web closes the circle by returning us to the 'city', no longer 'upon the hill' but safely behind the screen. Rather than constructing a virtual city, internet activity seems to render uniformity among the likeminded, a new type of atomisation strangely parallel to the gated villages of the middle landscape: an entire universe of overlapping archipelagos, sequestered behind firewalls and meeting the desires of narrow audiences. The sea change necessary to rally the citizenry around a common goal is literally up against these virtual walls. How can progressives break into these secluded domains? Those prepared for a campaign 'of building as natural as possible' must bridge the gap to the next step of the Giant Retro-Fit, squarely in the domain of urbanism and design.

Field & Stream

For the enormous energy driving the self-organising city to evolve, the metropolis must be divided in two. One half of this will be planned, built and managed by 'the government', and centred on 'infrastructure', the metropolitan flyways utilised by streams of people, goods and services. Realising this complex endeavour will necessarily require a coalition that over time will transform into a metropolitan partnership between the mayor, county judge, their offices and the communications industry. This is beyond the scope of the current political climate, but outlines of such a planning agency already exist in the form of TransStar, an unusual agency which brings state, city and county transportation agencies under one roof. The second half of the middle landscape is the holey plane, where self-organisation reigns, holding in its generous arms: gated communities, condos, lacunae of open fields, self-imposed flooding controls, in other words 80 per cent of the metropolitan world. A motley crew of developers navigate this field, closely observed by suburban villagers. Citizens navigate their own personal agendas through the turbulence, roughly following the rules of the open city. But for the field to function it must be accessible via metropolitan infrastructures containing the leftover alphabet soup: freeways, roads, regional parks, flooding districts, water and sewage, building codes and, now more than ever, the streams of communication run by giant telecommunications monopolies (AT&T and Google). Bundled together, these streams form the trunk lines of the metropolitan field. Holding them *apart* while remaining synchronised is the primary struggle for a self-organising middle landscape; striking a delicate balance between public and private.

The result of an ideal balance is an *embedded field*, where overlapping is organic – in the sense of complex tissue rather than mechanical stacking. Self-organisation in this context is like a bumper car operating in the fleshy part of the tissue, always constrained and waylaid by centrally controlled streams, in various manifestations from virtual to physically present. The bundle of infrastructure contains one strand concerning water and sewage, a metabolic couple straddling the gap between nature and artifice. This narrow domain ties together the canopy of trees, waterways and moist prairie, displaying a unification otherwise unknown on the diffuse field.

Putting this domain in public focus is both environmentally and politically astute. Management by a new agency of experts and citizens will ensure that it bridges between the self-organised and the governed, serving as a meeting ground upon which the public good is of central concern. The zoohemic solar pumps – with their crowns exposed to the heavens and their rhizomes infiltrating the prairie – are models for this new bundle of metabolic tissue and inspiration for the task ahead.

A case in point: the disastrous dealings with the potentially exquisite domain of bayous must be the most glaring example of collective denial. The bayous, essential for irrigation of the prairie, are even today relegated to the business of run-off – mere plumbing – while their rich and ecologically complex function is simply ignored. Citizens are very slowly realising that a certain beauty sleeps along the bayous, if not the future of the middle landscape itself. At the bayou, the necessity of a more effective infrastructure and the needs of the population must be productively combined. Historically, attempts to improve the bayous have derived inspiration from the forcibly manicured suburban landscape. But there exists an opportunity to produce an effective run-off system *and* a public amenity. The common good might be here pursued despite the bifurcation of responsibility in the otherwise self-organised city. The middle landscape is thus divided in two: field and stream (infrastructure), held together by a third entity – water and sewage. If it seems a bit bizarre, please bear with me!

The diffuse terrain – coursed through by mobility – lies before us: tattered, discontinuous, hopelessly interrupted. Any architect would aim to make it whole again. But that would betray nostalgia for masterplans as much as it would derail the experimental nature of the diffuse city. How can we advance this project without losing Houston's relative openness and unruly democracy, in which representatives are developers shadowed by a cadre of politicos? There is one potential avenue (with a huge rock in its path).

Private interest is the most fundamental socio-political character of Houston. Public interest appears mostly to encumber the entrepreneurial project.

The Giant Retro-Fit

The entrepreneurial project thrives on action, on growth and change. Now outside the field of action in the public domain, the delta of bayous has literally been relegated to the backwaters of the development equation. It is therefore a safe place to start a public revolution, radical only in an ecological sense. Convincingly presenting a system of unattractive run-off channels as a public asset of exceptional value will take some rhetorical skill. (A tenacious group of dedicated individuals has been at this for a long time, paddling up and down the bayous, without penetrating the field beyond.) Since the entire city is served by the delta, it should not be hard to argue its common relevance. Because it would be utopian to think the entire system could attain its former bucolic glory, the project must begin as a piecemeal experiment altering the uneasy relation between nature and culture. There must be a way to link a complex understanding of ecological systems to technology. Constructing a *hybrid* of the old (natural) bayou and a natural-ised public park system[3] would reverse one fundamental principle of what has been called landscape urbanism – namely, making a spectacle of the original ecology (while hiding the

3. In the *Houston Daily Post* of 24 August 1903, the reporter gushes about the new Highland Park on the bayou, featuring an artificial lake making use of waters from the bayou and an artesian well. Houstonians knew the ideal solution long before me – so much for progress.

247

necessary technology). Any idea that the bayou might be restored to its former state, or that there are no returns left, is negated by a hybrid bayou domain revealing the necessity of run-off systems and providing public amenity. With a renewed delta of bayous, Houstonians will realise that nature and culture can no longer be separated, but must be brought together with ever new complexity. Such a public awakening is critical to the revitalisation of the middle landscape.

Opposite the bayou, at the very heart of the diffuse city, is the subdivision: groomed, predictable, safe. The typical single-family house reached by broad, winding streets provides immediate pressure for change. Its every aspect is highly energy-dependent: poor insulation, single-glazed windows, excessive interior space blind to the solar path, excessive water use, air-conditioning. Even the slight elevation of the entire subdivision is designed to deliver excess run-off water outside – down the pike, not our responsibility. Not to speak of the oversized vehicle, the lawnmower, the dirt bike. All is ripe for retooling: insulation, triple-glazed windows, trombe walls, solar panels, the return of the porch and the fan, climate-zoned interiors, water conservation and recycling, ponds to collect roof runoff, hybrid cars, the bicycle. These adjustments are entirely feasible and energy-efficient, providing opportunity for innovation and new industry. In other words: private self-organising enterprise (underpinned by government).

Further out in the equation: in the past, hidden in deeds and mortgage agreements only brought to light at tax time, new concerns arise – sub-prime loans, bad debt, liquidity issues, bank closures – that when combined bring entire subdivisions to auction and then the abyss: *entire subdivisions are turned into rental property.* The American Dream as it is known ceases to exist – for an entire generation. Maybe forever. On a brighter note, the inhabitants of subdivisions (still gated, but inspired by the Giant Retro-Fit), may begin to understand themselves as members of a village with a shared destiny. Common space is sought – the primordial desire for a village green – and the awkward leftover lacuna uncomfortably connecting the next subdivision comes into focus. A hole in the holey plane has found a purpose; a public conversation has begun. And then more radically, public paths are cut at lot lines and across private property to reach the green. Suddenly the fence is gone, then most of the fences. Bobby can meet Sue without walking the streets. Public life returns and the subdivision as we have known it is history.

Next the villagers talk about the bayou, just a block away. There are meetings with the city, the architect to build a bicycle path, an ice house, a swimming pool right next to the pond still fouled by surface run-off (but this can be fixed too). The bayou domain has returned to the citizenry, the middle landscape has found its destiny.

Is it a scenario so farfetched? The sooner we begin the Giant Retro-Fit, the longer we can stretch the oil supply (predicted to run out within 50 years, with no viable alternative energy on the horizon). The most crucial aspect of technological retooling is that it brings public interests to the fore. Without it, the grand experiment of living in a diffuse city will fail.

By concentrating this design effort on the subdivision and two types of terra firma – the bayous and the gaps of undeveloped land – we have surreptitiously shifted from private interests to public. Since these holes in the field increase both in size and frequency the further away from the inner loop we move, the inner delta of bayous must be most intensively developed and those at Houston's outer edges less so. Many complexities are hidden in this proposal, from jurisdiction to ownership to financing to urgency to local predilections. The result would not be a traditional necklace of parks, but a chain of unique projects tied to each location. A design agency administering such a process, and supporting local environmental interests, would require jurisdiction – even eminent domain – to bind the broken down in-between into a network of open space. Herein lies another fallacy of landscape urbanism's enthusiasm: contiguity's mythical importance and a desire to frame the diffuse.[4] Contiguity is not important to the roaming subject (equipped with human analogues to slow motion, rewind, erase, jump-cut, juxtaposition and fast-forward technology) – access and utility are. Ours is a design project in which the complex of nature and culture must be synthesised; artificial ecology will be central to the new design enterprise zone. A geological shift in opinion must also take place: the self-oriented dweller must realise that the strangely shaped no-man's-land dividing his or her subdivision from the next is now under his or her jurisdiction – if it borders on a bayou, there is an even more complex project to hand. My speculation ends here, where it enters into the hands of a new public.

Oil-thinking

But we must return to that stumbling block on the road to utopia. As previously suggested, only a catastrophic situation will force a radical sea-change in public and political opinion. Why this peculiar stubborn resistance to the public good, or to regulation of any kind, instigated by neighbour, local or federal government? To understand this attitude of deep-seated aversion, we must revisit the oil gusher of 10 January

4. However my colleague, Malaysian architect Ken Yeang, has argued that physical interruption is destructive to the species-migration of a holistic environment – suggesting that environmental bridges or contiguity of habitat may well be essential.

1909 at Spindletop, near Beaumont, Texas some 90 miles from Houston. The moment marked 'a new era of civilisation' (as proclaimed by signs at the source). It is questionable whether this was in fact 'civilisation', since oil exploration along the south coast was reckless, euphoric, dangerous and wasteful of all natural resources necessary for the project of extraction. Spindletop, shooting hundreds of feet into the air, blew for weeks before it was tamed. In the meantime, oil leaked into the waterways and seeped into the aquifer to adversely affect the groundwater, maybe forever. As Joseph A Pratt eloquently discusses in 'A Mixed Blessing: Energy, Economic Growth, and Houston's Environment', what I refer to as 'oil-thinking' is fundamental to Houston's collective consciousness, colouring everything from the way Houstonians see themselves in relation to the city, to how the government reluctantly invades their privacy and equally reluctantly acts on the unforeseen consequences of oil pollution from the gusher to the excruciatingly slow commute through endless sprawl.[5] Oil-thinking has no time for reflection, no time for stasis; everything is invested in action, in unfettered forward thinking – freedom before caution.

The wild euphoria that exploded at Spindletop has been tempered by the ensuing tumult of the remainder of the twentieth century, but if there is such a thing as a psychological geology, giving a city and its citizens a central character, oil is it. The environmental history of Houston deeply explored by Melosi, Pratt et al, makes a strong case for distinctive cultural and economic underpinnings.[6] Oil money gave us the Texas Medical Center (M D Anderson). And Exxon financed

5. Joseph A Pratt, 'A Mixed Blessing: Energy, Economic Growth, and Houston's Environment' in Martin V Melosi and Joseph A Pratt (eds), *Energy Metropolis: An Environmental History of Houston and the Gulf Coast* (Pittsburgh, PA: University of Pittsburgh Press, 2007), 17–21.

some of the first suburban sprawl in the Friendswood area (and later Kingwood), while Woodlands was developed by oilman George Mitchell. Oil also drained and built the Houston Ship Channel in 1914, which later became one of the largest tanker ports in the world. Oil (natural gas and petroleum) built the highways, displaced the old railroads (and the coal that built *them*) and through refinement spawned the petrochemical industry. But at the advent of oil Houston was already accustomed to the exploration, refinement, sale and transportation of natural resources (cotton, lumber, sulphur, salt and rice), such that oil-thinking is even more basically, *natural resource thinking*. Therefore all the elements associated with oil transport are unquestioned: the pipelines, tanker trucks, barges, ships and the refineries that would make moviemakers giddy with their 'special effects', emitting ominous vapours and belching fire plumes into the night sky. Pollution is commonplace and not until the rattling sabre of regulation appears will the corporate captains and entrepreneur-developers wake up – at first to protest, then to lobby and broker backroom deals, but soon enough outdoing potential government regulation via self-regulatory measures (but only as long as whistle-blowers keep up the heat). As Pratt describes, spurts of self-regulation occurred frequently during the 'era of the gusher' (1909–1930) but slackened due to lack of public pressure during 'mounting pollution/under-regulation' (1920–1960).[7] In other words, the key motivator in the evolution of oil-thinking is to inspire good will, not to regulate. With a newfound territory centred on the delta of bayous and its outlying gaps of skipped-over green space, a vigilant public has the best chance to keep the agents of the field on the straight and narrow.

6. See Martin V Melosi and Joseph A Pratt's insightful introduction, ibid, 1–16.

7. Ibid, 26–41.

As Saskia Sassen has shown repeatedly in her work, it is at our own peril that we consider postwar cities like Atlanta, Dallas and Houston as entirely the same. In fact each city has a deep *material base* that has shaped its culture and economics over a very long time. It is therefore advantageous to see Houston as reflected in a huge oil-slick; though reserves may waste away within half a century, oil motivates below consciousness, resulting in a daily repertoire of Pavlovian responses: self-reliance, independence, action over reflection, government aversion, boosterism, endless progress... Despite undeniable spirit, without radical reorientation these qualities do not bode well for a future Houston *sans* oil.

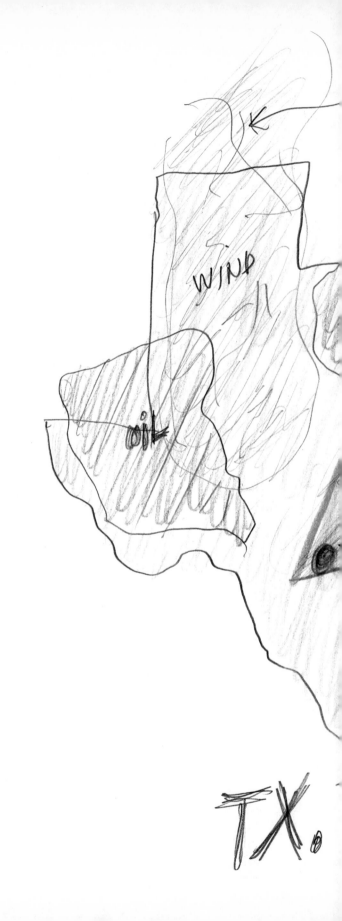

corrido

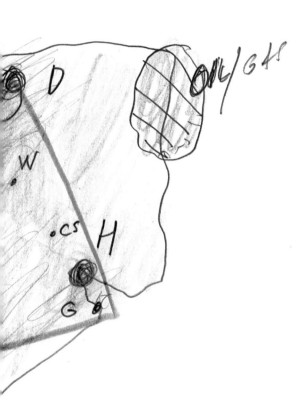

OIL/GAS

D

W

.cs   H

G

RIANGLE

The Dawn of Oil-Thinking

A recent rainstorm howling in from the northeast rapidly enshrouds the suddenly ghostly downtown megashape, obscures it, then makes it disappear. And then it reappears, as if a film were rewound. These tricks of illusion are common at my window. They are also graphic illustrations of the city's own economic ups and downs. At the point of this writing in the summer of 2009, it is hard to know if Houston is disappearing or appearing. The global economic doldrums remain opaque. A wider perspective than offered by my high-rise perch or high-speed view from the interstate may help.[1]

Houston's Fortune 500 companies are still here, many of them hiding behind gleaming facades downtown. Just before the downturn, Texas claimed a huge portion of the nation's job growth, much of which directly benefited Houston, partly propelled by hurricane Katrina in New Orleans. Today, recession has arrived in the form of layoffs and empty condominium towers, reminding of the 1980s, yet the unemployment rate in Texas is still two points below the national average. As often as not Houston faces political uncertainty: after the effective businessman mayor Bill White (who, like Jim Jones will go on to Washington), who will be in charge? A lawyer? How about an architect? When will there be a Hispanic candidate? Demographic changes suggest that Hispanics will soon dominate the political arena, giving it a Democratic stamp. But such speculation is based on homogenous profiling, which always leads to misjudgements.

In my view, the fact that Houston sees itself as energy capital of the world is more important for the city's *modus operandi* than either politics, race or gender. Underpinned by oil-thinking, liberal attitudes – in the true sense – influence

1. Of particular value here: 'Special Report on Texas: Lone Star Rising', *The Economist*, 11–17 July 2009.

the actions and self-conception of Houstonians. Self-reliance and responsibility for one's actions are favoured over government and are at the heart of the city's character. For example, gasoline prices. One would think a city with long commuting distances would champion cheap gas. Not so – rising gas prices are good for Houston's economy however bad for the nation. In the end, difference is what makes cities unique. Texas geography helps here; taken not only as a landmass but a multi-dimensional environment concerning not only what is buried below, but also what blows across its surface. First, the boundless prairie benefits the rugged individualism of oil-thinking. Second, the prairie is beginning to diversify. Suddenly huge wind turbines harness the steadily blowing wind, and natural gas championed (over gasoline) as fuel for various forms of transportation. The technological advances encouraged by scarcity expand the conception of the prairie's resources. Houston is no longer the lonely centre of petroleum but part of the 'Texaplex' (Texas x metroplex), which I prefer to call the Texas Triangle (including San Antonio, Dallas and Austin as a blue dot floating in a red sea). This convenient conception appeals to the myth and ambitions of Texas the Nation.[2] Diversification permeates the Triangle on local levels: Dallas is not just banking but also aerospace and distribution. Likewise San Antonio is not only next to Mexico and NAFTA, but closely bound to the military and the southern auto industry, as represented by Toyota. Infrastructural concerns make the Triangle a living reality, forcing Texans to contemplate not only new super highways but also high-speed rail and the expansion of the ERCOT power grid.[3] These acts of consolidation are technological as well as psychological.

2. 'Texaplex' was coined by David Winans (http://www.texaplex.com/).

3. The Electric Reliability Council of Texas (ERCOT) operates the electrical grid and manages the deregulated market

A strange symmetry exists in the correspondence between city-to-city infrastructure and village-making within the city, and the new connectivity across the prairie and consolidated character of each city. The 'frogs around the bayous' have multiplied into families of amphibians now feasting on various resources around the state.

Avoiding the nightmare scenario of a long-lasting and global depression, Houston still has serious problems that I have not covered here. Not only is there a need for political restructuring based on the schism dividing city and county, but a serious question about education.

With the shift from the extraction and refinement of oil products to include the push and pull of wind and gas (possibly supplemented by clean coal and nuclear power) there is an urgent need for knowledge-workers in Texas.[4] Yet the state has preferred to export its knowledge-hungry to schools elsewhere in the nation, hoping for their eventual return, while at times importing others. Tales of the blatant purchase of doctors to operate Texas Medical Center date back to the 1950s. Whatever the outcome of these demographic shifts, highly educated Texans will demand serious revitalisation of preparatory education. The other contingency of new Texans – a steady flow of the under-educated – seeking low-paid jobs for themselves but better for their children, will push education to the front of the political agenda. This leads us back to oil-thinking.

Looking briefly at the dramatic technological demands of oil extraction, the pressure for change seems obvious. The oil prospector roaming the geological surface has been replaced by the virtual prospector commanding a bank of computers, marking a shift in the foundations of oil-thinking from the actual to the virtual, from symptomatic to almost-factual (even

4. 'Lone Star Rising', *op cit*, p 4.

'facts' can lie since they arrive on screen as approximations). Likewise the working conditions and skills of workers in the field have changed dramatically since the time of the old roughnecks. Has oil-thinking changed accordingly? The lack of concern for education, all across the state, suggests that it has not.

Recent changes in the oil industry suggest that renewed education in this field – beyond the further education provided by companies to retain their 'best people' – is an opportunity that could encompass an expanded view of energy including wind, solar, gas, coal and nuclear. With a wealth of local oil-technologists operating small companies, Houston is spawning the next phase of oil-thinking, necessary to move up the energy ladder. Here a domino arrangement of preparatory education in community colleges linked directly to local universities could have a cumulative effect, and influence attitudes toward education across Texas. But the obstacles to this are formidable. The windmills erected in the Texas wind corridor are made in Europe, with blades from Siemens and parts from Spain's Acciona.[5] As with so many alternative technologies, windmill towers and solar cells are produced in countries with expensive energy bills including Japan, Germany and the Netherlands. (Unlike Germany, technology was never a strongpoint – the German immigrants who came early to Texas were farmers, not refugees from the industrial Ruhrgebiet.) Houston's oil-thinking must be radically revamped to compete in a global arena. Suppose the link between space-technology and superconductivity developed at the University of Houston (electrical conductivity can be radically improved at low temperatures) generates research

5. See *Wind Energy Resource Atlas of the United States*, at http://rredc.nrel.gov/wind/pubs/atlas/chp3.html#s_central

interests matching those of space and oil to tackle our enormous need for electricity? Speculation about drawing coal into the petroleum equation (specifically, the large quantities of carbon dioxide released from new onsite clean coal plants)[6] reveals that a mixed energy picture of oil, gas, wind, solar and coal *is* coming into focus, allowing many previously peripheral industries to enter energy production. The reinvention of the energy-supply-chain[7] is underway, now multi-linked, stressing *connectivity* rather than the traditional petroleum monopoly characteristics of isolation and exclusivity. Dependencies between oil-states, now challenged by a global energy supply market, make everyone a potential link. Diplomacy over energy wars, crowdsourcing (the mixing and matching of many energy sources) over corporate monoculture.[8]

According to research at the Brookings Institution, suburban job-growth far exceeds that of dense centralised cities (while symmetrically having the highest unemployment rates in times of recession).[9] This suggests that the county, the vibrant heart of the middle landscape, can foster pockets of high-tech education, closely linked to Houston's shop culture. There is a further argument for suburban village formation, since historically not only housing but work and leisure were

6. BP's version of injecting CO2 into oil wells: Injecting natural gas is one way of flushing more oil out of a well. Tests have shown that carbon dioxide, which can be separated from oil and other hydrocarbons during hydrogen power production, may be an effective substitute. Putting this CO2 back into the reservoir means it won't be released into the atmosphere, where it would add to the greenhouse gases believed to cause global warming. http://www.bp.com/sectiongenericarticle.do?categoryId=9021505&contentId=7040002

7. Ed Burghard of Harley Procter Marketer writes: 'The US manufacturing industry is in the midst of a long and sometimes difficult transition. As globalisation leads to lower-cost production of mainstream products, American manufacturers must re-apply their world-class expertise in old-line processes to emerging technologies. This process is rapidly accelerating in the advanced energy supply chain, which promises to lessen US dependence on unstable foreign energy markets while establishing a foundation for a thriving domestic clean-energy industry.' Ed Burghard, 'New US Energy Supply Chain', *Industry Week*, 27 July 2009 http://www.industryweek.com/articles/new_u-s_energy_supply_chain_19643.aspx

8. See Jeff Howe, 'The Rise of Crowdsourcing', *Wired*, June 2006, 42.

9. See Paul Sommers and Drew Osborne, 'Middle-Wage Jobs in Metropolitan America', especially *The Brooking Institution: Metropolitan Economy Initiative* 9, 10 June 2009.

closely integrated. Promoting consolidation in the decentralised domains, such a development might even please the inquisitive glares of what Joel Kotkin calls the *Torquemadas* (Militant Greens), named after the first Spanish inquisitor. The consequence of such a radical revitalisation of education would lead to a veritable Texas Energy Triangle dispersed all throughout the middle landscape, including expanded city boundaries in the 'wind corridor' of Western Texas and cities like Odessa (the true extraction capital of the Permian Basin). For a century, oil-thinking has rested comfortably in entrepreneurial 'roughneck' mode. Both state and individual cities have relied on its local economy and therefore remained globally insignificant. To open the door to the energy triangle we must rapidly recognise the fundamental connection between global reach, entrepreneurship and education. Herein lies the true challenge.

Closely connected, in fact, to industry is the city's liveability. There are two distinctly vulnerable populations in Houston, inhabiting opposite ends of the spectrum: the future knowledge-worker, who demands services and a high standard of living, and the poor, who require education, stability and an extensive support system. Additions at either end of the spectrum pose challenges. Joel Kotkin suggests that the future liveability of a suburban city such as Houston revolves around three preoccupations: public safety, business climate and political reform.

'Business climate' is not a problem for Houston, as has been shown by developers and their flexible real-estate market, as well as the rapid absorption into the labour pool of Katrina refugees. The concern for public safety most visibly displayed in the gated community is a psychological issue. Safety is a perceived concern among the well-to-do and a real concern in areas of poverty. Kotkin writes: 'These areas could stage a real resurgence if their governments determine to throttle criminals, improve basic services and mature small business'.[10] This opportunity is particularly striking in Houston's inner loop, where land in the vulnerable wards is still cheap and abundant, and often located near bustling megashapes. Such are the 'positive' side effects of no zoning and leapfrogging, allowing 'cumbersome wards' to remain almost intact. With the insertion of workplaces and educational satellites the wards could begin to undo chronically unproductive conditions. As a recent review of our state suggests: 'How Texas responds to these forces will determine its future'.[11]

In my view, 'these forces' pose an enormous challenge to the idea of Houston, and unless future agents of change tread lightly, the city may become the victim of its own success. The most vulnerable characteristic of this vibrant place is its self-organisation. Oil-thinking is its primary motor, that with its newfound weaknesses could easily be dismissed as old Texas. But that would be a fatal mistake. Houston is a twentieth-century experiment in habitation, work and leisure of a third kind, facing new and demanding challenges in the twenty-first century.

10. Joel Kotkin, 'America's (Sub)urban Future', *Forbes*, 5 May 2009.
11. 'Lone Star Rising', op cit, 4.

On Ill
Winds and
Fool's Gold

Wearily, we Houstonians follow tropical storms brewing over the Atlantic. When one takes shape – revealing an eye after having raced across the Caribbean Sea to the Gulf of Mexico – we nervously stock up. Between forays for water, canned food and batteries, we watch reports of route speculation and listen to hurricane trackers. At these moments Houstonians are reminded that despite the city's prominence and size, it is also a tiny target in the planet's giant climate factory. Favourable conditions in the troposphere produce a steering wind; combined with ocean temperature and solar power, a gigantic centrifuge hurls towards the oil capital of the world.

Begun in Africa, pushed along the trade winds then held tightly in place between a hot sea and cold stratosphere, the radical temperature differences buoy the storm west. South of Cape Verde the turbulence gets organised, is named and begins to wreak havoc: Puerto Rico, the Dominican Republic, Haiti, Cuba and the Cayman Islands. Slightly winded and now gendered (Allison or Hugo), the storm catches its breath – regaining strength when it reaches the Gulf proper.

On 13 September 2008 Hurricane Ike hit us dead-on.

Months later, catastrophe contractors are still refurbishing the last of the 169 battered (of 209) apartments in my high-rise. Most suffered water damage and an occasional blown-out window; no one was injured. My 18th-floor perch was untouched.

Ike arrived at night. Unlike an earthquake – an under-ground freight train that suddenly rushes through the earth's crust – a hurricane is a geological and molecular event. The noise cataclysmic.

A hurricane warns, teases, builds, wavers, halts, pushes forward, forms, and then acquires a semi-hypothetical rating. The meterologists keep us awake, waiting for something to report – as if it were a giant sporting event. They fly in and out, measuring atmospheric pressure and wind speed on a giant centrifuge that separates the flotsam and jetsam from the fixed. The mayor appears on television: 'This is going to be a bad one, evacuate the following zip codes…' Then the landfall.

Ike is a pedagogical storm. Almost human, he knows left from right, east from west. His eye – an immense socket of emptiness (in which you can hear the birds sing again) churning through the middle of the storm. When Ike hits Galveston his path is roughly set, he knows what he is up to. As a 'category 2', Ike indiscriminatingly clears the east side of the island, while mostly sparing the more inhabited west side. His message to the islanders is to move back inland. *This is my domain: the oceans, the pounding surf, the marshes and the wetlands – the littoral.*

When Ike hits us 'hunkered down' in central Houston, he has been building up with sudden bursts of wind and rain, frazzled and incoherent at the outer edges. With a sustained wind force Ike shakes everything. Windows shudder; the metal fence some five feet away rattles and screeches as nature's instrument. I descend from the 18th floor to the 3rd-floor apartment of a colleague. When the lights go out, first indecisively, then for a week, we realise that we are not prepared – so much for warnings and college degrees. (Not even a flashlight.) Peeking out of the windows, we spy a large metal hulk, a giant helmet, wedged between the building and the metal fence: a sheet metal ventilation cap from two buildings down. It might have gone through the window…

With generators that have power for just three hours the elevators soon break down, the dark stair cores are impassable and with no fire alarms, the building is shut down. We are asked to evacuate. The first fallen tree, outside the entrance to our high-rise, is startling. (As we soon realise, just one of many thousands.) A beautiful oak spread-eagled across the street tells us that even the glorious zoohemic canopy, planted by Houstonians, is not ours but nature's frontier. Driving towards campus, we dodge obstacles, are forced to stop, turn around, as if the city has suddenly become a labyrinth. There is a new hesitancy, a new politesse totally uncharacteristic of a citizenry accustomed to never slowing down, running both yellow and red. Again the fallen trees and with them electric lines hanging listlessly and dead to the street from ragged poles.

Hurricanes, and tornadoes, are known to punish the weak more severely than the rich and powerful; trailer parks being a favourite target (though Ike did remind the city's gardeners that their meticulous pruning can be undone in one long night). But Ike's communiqué to the 'power elite' – the Captains of Industry, City Fathers, Downtown Types – is that everyone is poor in the face of nature's wrath. As if to make a final point, half of the lower windows in the Chase Tower are blown out. (One of banks left standing through the financial turmoil racing across the entire world is taught a different lesson here.) Although science will tell us that the blown-out windows were some bizarre coincidence of Venturi effect, wind-speed and building morphology, we know it was in fact a message.

Will we learn from Ike? Will we bury the electrical infra- structure even if it promises to be a 20-year project costing billions? (Unless we can jump directly to cordless.) Probably not, even though the last two storms cost Houston $3 billion and Ike will cost more than double. No, what we will remem- ber is our momentary return to the nineteenth century and the sudden neighbourliness. In feeble attempts to return to our own time, electrical cords stretched for blocks to keep refrigerators alive among those of us who lost power. We celebrate our own foolish tenacity at the Gulf Coast, because we will rebuild.

For the urbanist, Ike meant something special: several years ago I wrote an illustrated scenario of a 500-year storm which surfaced earlier in this book, but I completely overlooked the vulnerability of the power grid, subject to the hurricane in collusion with the canopy. Disease, rain, fire, looting, bayou flooding, refinery closures I accounted for, but not the most obvious weakness of the system: the electrical lines awkwardly weaving through the oaks, the current driving the gas and diesel pumps that motivate the suburban city. (And the pumps that supply fuel to privately owned generators, no longer able to defend even Houston's wealthiest patrons.) Dick Tracy was half-right when he exclaimed: 'The one who owns the sewage owns the city.'

For Houstonians, Ike prefigured the current calamity which appears climatic – on the scale of global warming – but now takes the shape of an economic storm. Houston has always been slow to catch on (gas prices are back under $2 per gallon and the highways at their normal ebb and flow). Perhaps we may prefer to see Ike as a statistic probability that will lessen the possibility of a Mamie to follow.

Looking out from my 18th-floor window – while listening to the concrete tower that has become an instrument in the hands of contractors chipping away at its problems – all I see are blue FEMA tarpaulins dotting the entire Houston panorama, covering roofs that have not yet been repaired after Ike. I wonder if each of those blue markers not only traces Ike, but might also signal the presence of a sub-prime mortgage, now in the eye of an economic hurricane...

While global economic turbulence worsens rapidly, Ike is forgotten. Many months later the blue tarpaulins remain, true indicators of repairs foreclosed; not undertaken. The incessant energy that egged me – and this book – along is sputtering, grinding slowly to an eerie conceptual halt. Optimism is stalled.

Even in the energy capital of the world there is hesitancy. Although cars on the freeway below me still drive on, the two gleaming glass towers across from the white-collar prisons are in receivership. At night I can see the anxiety of the new condo owners lit up in lonely windows, widely dispersed along their facades like houses in a subdivision. Around us are layoffs and budget cuts. I reluctantly feel my own spell of the Stockholm syndrome fading, in a small measure of disloyalty for my object of affection. It is a wake-up call for the suburban city.

Normally sphinx-like, the middle landscape for a brief moment reveals its darkest secrets. In this sudden lucidity, held still by economic slowdown, is there an arch in the proscenium – revealing a new stage for the national project? Houston was only just the final stage of the American Dream – snoozing satisfactorily in a million cul-de-sacs – as a city, 'a body without organs' whose opaque surface conceals unfulfilled potential. What 'desire machines' are necessary to break the somnolence of the endless horizon, to set the actors and their accoutrements in action, again? Perhaps: public works, preserving the holey plane or rejuvenating the bayous, as 'waterworks' for all?

How does such an awakening take place?

Fast forward to May 2010. A huge oil spill in the Gulf destroying the beloved littoral: the hunting grounds, the waterways, the wetlands. Is the very earth erupting? The same earth that Texans daily penetrate with greed and great skill? Striated catacombs pulsing with black gold (measured in pints and gallons in the everyday) haemorrhage their last. Is this the final challenge to oil-thinking – its ritual death? When will we realise *this* is the real issue – not weather, not global warming, not bank fraud. Houston is poster child for this truly majestic drama of human occupation. The same urban eyes blinded by the mantra 'mere sprawl' will continue their rejection of suburbia.[1] Houstonians must prove that the city of the third kind is the robust other of the dense city. In short, citizens awake!

But I hear a whisper from the self-organising city: there is no 'citizenry', no potential collective awakening. You forget that when Houstonians face a challenge – economic or environmental – a myriad of individual forces and occasional pragmatic coalitions adjust, move, sidestep, advance, and come to terms. Not exactly in unison but by 'hook and crook' to eventually end up on the other side – swarming rather than planned attack. And oil-thinking is always one of its many motors. It may still have mileage left.

1. The physicist Geoffrey West, whose hard numbers add robustness to those who believe in 'rules that govern everything', has added new ammunition for the dense city. As a sceptic I have more faith in a biological concept of the city, undeniably affected by West's 'mathematics' but given impetus by the specific metabolic character of each city. Furthermore, I have ideological problems with a suggestion that there may be underlying 'techniques of domination' resulting from unintended co-functioning of urban technologies themselves. I am much more inclined to the Foucauldian notion that 'techniques of the self' are the ultimate drivers of the self-organising city.